BUS

ACPL ITEM

DISCARDED

3 1833 03988 76

S0-BWW-677

Bankroll Your Future Retirement

"This book should be required reading for every American expecting to get old. For today's young adults in particular—who will bear the brunt of the Baby Boomer age wave and would do well to prepare themselves now—everything they need to know is in Ellen Hoffman's terrific and lucid book."

—Richard Thau, Executive Director, Third
Millennium, co-author, *Get It Together by 30*

"Ellen Hoffman's book is filled with lists and important telephone numbers and addresses, for both government and private programs for those planning for retirement. It is really a toolbox for those near retirement and those far from retirement, but eager to plan ahead."

—Martha Priddy Patterson, author,
The Working Woman's Guide to Retirement Planning

"This is an invaluable resource for women planning their retirement. Women of every age need to know more about the importance of Social Security, Medicare, and pension savings to their retirement security."

—Congresswoman Barbara Kennelly, Ranking Minority Member,
Social Security Subcommittee, US House of Representatives

"Ellen Hoffman is one of the most realistic finance writers around."   —*Dallas Morning News*

"Everyone over the age of 21 should read this book. In one easy-to-read volume, Ellen Hoffman has created a road map that both current and future retirees can follow—starting now—to make the best of the myriad of federal policies that have an impact on our golden years."

—Anne Werner, President & CEO,
United Seniors Health Cooperative

Other Books by Ellen Hoffman
The Retirement Catch-Up Guide
How to Plan a Successful Trip
Time Traveler's Guide: Columbus' Spain

BANKROLL YOUR FUTURE RETIREMENT
With Help From Uncle Sam

*How Government Perks and Policies
Can Affect Your Income, Your Healthcare,
Your Home, and Your Assets*

SECOND EDITION

ELLEN HOFFMAN

Newmarket Press   New York

Copyright © 1999, 2001 by Ellen Hoffman
(Previously titled *Bankroll Your Future*, ISBN 1-55704-355-8)

This book is published in the United States of America.

All rights reserved. This book may not be reproduced, in whole or in part, in any form, without written permission. Inquires should be addressed to: Permissions Department, Newmarket Press, 18 East 48th Street, New York, NY 10017.

Second Edition

10 9 8 7 6 5 4 3 2 1

Library of Congress Cataloging-in-Publication Data
Hoffman, Ellen, 1943–
Bankroll your future retirement with help from Uncle Sam / Ellen Hoffman.—2nd ed.
p. cm.
Rev. ed. of : Bankroll your future : how to get the most from the government for your retirement years— / Ellen Hoffman.
Includes bibliographical references and index.
ISBN 1-55704-462-7 (pbk. : alk. paper)
1. Retirement income—United States—Planning.   2. Social security—United States.
3. Medicare.   4. Aged—Long-term care.   5. Housing—United States.   6. Finance, Personal—Aged.   I. Hoffman, Ellen, 1943- Bankroll your future.   II. Title.
HD7125 .H567   2001
332.024'01—dc21   2001030311

Quantity Purchases
Companies, professional groups, clubs, and other organizations may qualify for special terms when ordering quantities of this title. For information, write Special Sales, Newmarket Press, 18 East 48th Street, New York, NY 10017, call (212) 832-3575, or fax (212) 832-3629.

Designed by Robert C. Olsson

Manufactured in the United States of America

CONTENTS

ACKNOWLEDGMENTS

Translating the complex, technical information that inevitably attaches to federal government programs into comprehensible language that is useful to the general public is a daunting task. It is all too easy for simplification to lead to subtle distortions or inaccuracies. That is why I am so grateful to a number of experts who volunteered their time to help me with this book.

I especially appreciate the assistance of the following people, who took the time to read and review some or all of various chapters of the book. Unless otherwise noted, all are from Washington, D.C.: Joe Baker, associate director of the Medicare Rights Center in New York; Bronwyn Belling of the Home Equity Information Center of the American Association of Retired Persons (AARP); Katherine Brod of the American Association of Homes and Services for the Aging; Stephanie Edelstein of the American Bar Association; Walter Feldesman, a New York attorney who wrote the *Dictionary of Eldercare Terminology*; Dean Graybill, an attorney at the Federal Trade Commission; Tom Margenau, with the Social Security Administration in San Diego; Tricia Neuman, director of the Medicare policy project for the Kaiser Family Foundation; Martha Priddy Patterson of KPMG Peat Marwick; L. Stephen Platt, partner at Arnold and Kadjan in Chicago; Michael Stern, a legislative representative for the Investment Company Institute; and Peggy Twohig, assistant director for credit practices at the Federal Trade Commission.

Many other people, both in and out of government, also gave generously of their time and advice. Among these government officials are Olena Berg, Joe Canary, and Sharon Morrissey at the U.S. Department of Labor; Judy Welles at the Pension

Benefit Guaranty Corp.; John Trollinger at the Social Security Administration; Sam Miller at the Health Care Financing Administration; and Gaela Bynum at the Department of Housing and Urban Development. Non-government experts who were generous with their help included Sally Dunaway and Cathy Ventrell-Monsees of the AARP, Gail Shearer of Consumers Union, Nicole Gudzowsky of the national Citizens Coalition for Nursing Home Reform, Chuck Mondin of United Seniors Health Cooperative, Geraldine Dallek of Families USA, Trish Nemore of the National Senior Citizens Law Center, financial planners Scott Kahan of New York and Robert F. Keats of Phoenix, and tax lawyer Jane Bruno and Margarita Provenzano for helping update these sections.

Tom Otwell of the AARP receives my special thanks for being the first to imagine me as the author of a book on retirement planning, as does Ann Eden for helping to find and organize materials for the "For More Information" sections of each chapter.

I also thank Henry Weil, my editor at *Retire With Money* newsletter published by *Money* magazine, for being a patient but demanding mentor; publisher Esther Margolis and editors Keith Hollaman, Rachel Reiss and Michelle Howry for their moral as well as professional support throughout this project; and Richard Accurso, with whom I look forward to enjoying my own retirement.

Note to the Reader: This publication is designed to provide accurate and authoritative information in regard to the subject matter covered. It is published with the understanding that the publisher and author are not engaged in rendering legal, accounting, or other professional services. If legal advice or other professional advice, including financial, is required, the services of a competent professional person should be sought.

Because criteria and rules for federal programs can change at any time, it is especially important for people to secure current information before trying to make decisions about any of the programs or policies described in this book.

This book contains many examples of how people's personal retirement situations are affected by federal programs and policies. In the cases where both first and last names are used, these are true examples. Where only a first name is used, the example has been created to illustrate a key point.

INTRODUCTION

Whether you like it or not, Uncle Sam will have an impact on your retirement.

When to stop working, how to invest your money, which doctor to choose, and where to live may appear to be highly personal retirement decisions to be made only by you and your family.

Yet, whether you are twenty-five or sixty-five, when you make decisions about your retirement, there is another silent but powerful partner in the room: the federal government.

We all know that what happens to the endangered Social Security and Medicare programs will have an impact on our retirement incomes and the quality of our retirement lives. But as important as they are, Social Security and Medicare represent only a *fraction* of the federal policies and programs that help determine your retirement income. Most of us have no idea what these policies are and how significant they can be to our future.

To ensure a comfortable retirement, today's savvy consumer must start making intelligent decisions as many as thirty years before he or she expects to leave the work force. Why?

• Social Security and Medicare are in trouble, and we cannot count on them to meet all of our basic retirement needs.

• Less than half of all private sector workers have private pensions.

• Downsizing and early retirement have swelled the ranks of workers who are self-employed and/or operating small businesses. Other than Social Security, the only retirement income they will have is what they save—and whatever earnings accrue to those savings—during their working years.

• Government policies that have created 401(k)s and similar plans have shifted the burden of retirement savings—and investment decisions—to the individual.

• "Retirement" is increasingly being defined as a career change, often to working part-time, as opposed to making a permanent departure from the work force.

All of these trends and policy changes are influenced by and embedded in policies made and carried out by the federal government. Depending on your work history, your financial status, your family situation, and your own knowledge of the system, the impact of the federal government on your retirement will be either positive or negative. The best strategy for achieving positive effects is to inform yourself about the government policies and programs that may touch your life, and to make informed decisions based on that knowledge.

In recent years, Congress has passed and the President has signed into law hundreds of changes in tax and other policies that may make a difference in your life when you retire. Do you know what these laws are and how to make the most of them?

Do you know what you can do to maximize your Social Security retirement benefit? If you have retiree health insurance from your employer, should you sign up for Medicare at age sixty-five? Can your employer force you to retire earlier than you want to because of your age? Should you give your financial assets to your children so that Medicaid will pay for your nursing home care? How can you tell if your pension money is safe? If you want to buy a retirement cottage in Tuscany, can you deduct the mortgage interest from your taxes? These are some of the questions you will find answered in this book.

Since I wrote the first edition of *Bankroll Your Future Retirement* in 1999, the need of baby boomers and others to find answers to these questions has struck me in a powerful way. The need is well-documented in my other book, *The Retirement Catch-Up Guide*, showing how fifty-four real people are trying now to adjust their finances to make up for lost time in saving for retirement. Failing to learn about the rules on issues such as Social Security and taxes are prominent reasons that many of the people interviewed for *The Retirement Catch-Up Guide* are scurrying now to provide for their retirement.

In sum: The purpose of the book is to bring Uncle Sam out of the shadows and into your conscious retirement planning—to help you make the right decisions starting now, regardless of your age. The case examples and practical checklists throughout the book will help you sort through what is often very technical, confusing information to get an idea of which policies may affect you and how you can make the best decisions for yourself and your family.

Bankroll Your Future Retirement is divided into three sections. In the first section, "Your Retirement Income," you'll find chapters on Social Security, pension policy, other retirement savings programs such as Individual Retirement Accounts, and laws that prohibit age discrimination in employment. The second section, "Promoting and Maintaining Your Health," describes how Medicare works, outlines Medicaid and other policies that affect nursing home care, and explains other health benefits such as those provided by the Veterans Administration and the new Medical Savings Accounts. The third section, "The Long Arm of the Law," contains chapters on other key areas of federal policy—programs and tax policies that may influence your decision on where to live in retirement, and consumer protections for retirees. To help you think through your own retirement plans, each chapter contains the following useful sections:

What You Need to Know:
A description of the policy requirements and benefits.

Decisions You Need to Make:
A list of questions to ask yourself about the potential impact of the policy on your retirement.

The Tax Factor:
How the choices you make about Social Security and other federal programs will affect your tax bill.

For More Information:
How to get more (mostly free) information about the policy—
by phone, by mail, and by searching the Internet.

Politicians are fond of saying that they oppose "big government" and that government should "stay out of people's lives."
But government is already firmly implanted in our retirement
lives. Without Uncle Sam, there would be no Social Security, no
Medicare, no 401(k) plans, no standards for nursing homes, and
no income tax deductions. These are not perfect policies, but
they are the law of the land.

It's totally up to you and your family to decide whether you
want to take advantage of these policies and programs. Before
this book was published, a friend of mine read the section on
maximizing Social Security benefits and, as a result, figured out
that he should retire at age sixty-two instead of waiting until
sixty-five.

My hope is that every reader of this book will find at least
one tip or piece of information that in some small way will contribute to improving her or his golden years. And if you do, I
hope that you will tell me about it by writing to me in care of
my publisher.

—Ellen Hoffman

A Word About Taxes

Are you working and saving for your future retirement?

Are you retired from a previous job or career, but still working, either at a new job or for yourself?

Are you fully retired?

No matter which category you fall into, Uncle Sam's tax policies are probably having a big impact on your current or future retirement income. Do you know what that impact is? Are you aware of all of the tax breaks that may reduce your taxes and of the penalties that could cut into your income?

Making significant financial decisions without considering their tax consequences is just plain foolhardy and may deprive you of present or future income.

In plotting the organization of this book, I originally envisioned devoting one chapter to addressing federal tax issues. But two things became increasingly clear:

• Such a chapter might end up as half or more of the book; and

• Tax policy is so enmeshed with other government policies that for the most part, they cannot be discussed separately.

That's why almost every chapter in this book has a special section called "The Tax Factor." In addition, at the end of the book you will find three checklists you can use to make sure you are aware of both the benefits and pitfalls of federal tax policy for your retirement.

PART ONE

YOUR RETIREMENT INCOME

CHAPTER ONE

Taking Control of Your Social Security Benefits

- Millie Johnson is sixty-seven and her husband George is sixty-nine. Together, they receive monthly Social Security benefits totaling $1,215.
- Joe, a bachelor all of his life, is sixty-nine. His monthly payment is $1,357.
- Dorothy, who has never worked outside her home, became a widow five years ago. At seventy-one years old, she receives $624 per month, less than three-fourths of the amount her husband would receive if he were alive.

Why does an individual, Joe, receive a bigger check than a couple, the Johnsons? Why does Dorothy, who is also not married, receive only half as much as Joe? What accounts for the discrepancies in the Social Security benefits of these retirees?

These are not the mistakes of a faceless bureaucrat. Starting with your first job, the choices you make about your employment status and family status may influence the amount of the benefits you can collect as many as forty years later.

Virtually every working American is eligible for Social Security retirement benefits, and more than 90 percent of current retirees receive them. But as you can see from the above examples, not all Social Security benefits are equal. We've all heard stories about retirees whose benefits support them comfortably on a tropical island or in a quaint mountain retreat. But we've also heard of recipients who face a grim daily struggle to stretch their benefit to cover rent, food, and utilities—to say nothing of medical and other unavoidable expenses.

Which scenario is more likely to represent your own retirement? Do you know how much Social Security retirement income you will receive? Or, if you are already retired, are you sure that you're getting the highest payment for which you are eligible?

Some factors that determine the size of your Social Security benefit—such as the death of your spouse or a recession—are beyond your control. But that is no excuse to passively assume that Social Security will just "happen" to you, or that it is something over which you have no influence. That's simply not true.

Social Security does not have the same impact on every retired person. That's why—whether you are retired or close to retirement, or you are thirty years old and not thinking about retirement at all—now is the time to check up on your Social Security. Given current uncertainties about the financial stability of the system, the longer you wait, the less Social Security income you may have to rely on in your golden years. This chapter will give you the basic information you need to secure the maximum Social Security benefits you deserve, whether you are eligible for them now or will be in the future.

WHAT YOU NEED TO KNOW ABOUT SOCIAL SECURITY BENEFITS

Taking control of your Social Security basically requires two steps: understanding the basic rules for calculating your benefit, and informing yourself about some little-known but effective steps you might take to boost the benefit as high as possible.

WHAT RETIREMENT BENEFITS YOU CAN EXPECT

The average monthly Social Security benefit for a retired worker at the end of 1999 was $898.60 for a man and $697.70 for a woman. The average monthly benefit for a couple in which the wife received a benefit based on her husband's work record was $1,356.80.

Each December, the government adjusts Social Security benefits to reflect inflation. This change, called a "cost of living adjustment" (COLA), becomes effective in January benefit pay-

The Future of Social Security

Should you be worried about the rumors that Social Security is going bankrupt? Could this happen in your lifetime?

The Board of Trustees of the Social Security Trust Fund—the account in which benefits are stored until they are distributed—has said that, unless fundamental changes are made in the program, as of 2037 the Fund will not have enough money to pay all the benefits that would be owed under the present system. At that time, the Trustees reported in 2000, the Trust Fund would still be able to pay about 72 percent of the benefits owed under the present system. As matters stand now, the resources in the trust fund will decline more rapidly in coming years, as baby boomers (people born from 1945 to 1965) start collecting Social Security and the number of younger workers available to contribute to the fund declines.

Both the amount of your potential benefit and the rules that determine how much you get could change, making a big difference in your retirement resources.

Numerous proposals have been offered to improve the long-term financial security of the Trust Fund, but no significant decisions are expected for at least a couple of years. One thing you can count on, however, is that Congress and the President are unlikely to cut or decrease the benefits of current retirees or those eligible for retirement in the next few years. So if you are in your early fifties or older, you can assume that you will receive more or less the same level of benefits as workers who already get Social Security. If you are younger than fifty, however, you definitely should pay close attention to the Social Security debate, because some of the proposals under consideration could erode your future benefits.

In this time of uncertainty, the best way to ensure that you'll have adequate retirement income is to take advantage of your access to a private pension plan and/or put as much money as possible into tax-deferred savings, such as a 401(k) plan or Individual Retirement Accounts, so that you will not need to rely entirely on Social Security.

ments. The COLA for 2001 is 3.5 percent. In 2000, the adjustment provided a benefit increase of 2.4 percent.

Several other factors influence the amount of your benefit: your retirement age, the number of years you worked, how much you earned, and your family or marital status. Here are the basics:

Retirement Age

The "full retirement age," at which you can draw the highest benefits, is sixty-five for people who were born in 1937 or earlier. If you were born later, your full retirement age will start somewhere between sixty-five and sixty-seven, depending on exactly how old you are. (See Chart 1-A, p. 24.)

You may start collecting benefits as early as age sixty-two, but there's a catch: if you go on Social Security anytime before your full retirement age, you'll get a lower benefit *for the rest of your life.* Currently, if you retire at sixty-two, your benefit will be cut 20 percent, permanently. The size of the cut declines the longer you wait. If you retire at age sixty-four, for example, the benefit reduction will be 6⅔ percent. If you retire between the ages of sixty-five and seventy, the longer you delay, the higher your benefit will be. (See Chart 1-B, p. 25.)

If you were born in 1960 or later, your full retirement age is sixty-seven, not the current sixty-five. In that case, your penalty for starting to collect benefits at age sixty-two will be even greater—a full 30 percent.

Work History

To qualify for Social Security, you must have worked and contributed to the system through payroll or FICA tax by earning a minimum amount of money ($3,320 in 2001) in each of ten years. You do not have to earn these credits consecutively. For example, you might work in an office for three years, then take a year of maternity or paternity leave before returning to employment. *If you do not meet these requirements, you will not be entitled to a Social Security retirement benefit,* unless your current, former, or deceased spouse meets or met the minimum requirement.

To calculate your Social Security benefit, Uncle Sam uses a formula based on your highest earnings for each of thirty-five years. For every year less than thirty-five that you have worked, there will be a zero in the calculation, which will reduce your yearly average and result in a lower benefit.

Family Status

If you are married, and you and your spouse both worked, you are each eligible for the highest benefit possible based on your own working record. In the case of George and Millie on p. 9, for example, $620 per month of the total $1,215 they receive is based on George's full-time work as a salesman. The additional $595 per month comes from Millie's intermittent and part-time work, teaching for a few years before they had their children and working part-time in a dress shop after the children grew up.

When only one spouse has worked outside the home, the other may receive a benefit equal to one half of what the worker gets at full retirement age. So if Millie had not worked at all, she and George would receive only $1,080 per month ($720 for George, and half of that, or $360, for Millie) instead of over $1,200.

One factor that does *not* affect your eligibility or the amount of your Social Security benefit is retirement income from other sources. The income you get from a private pension, personal savings, or your savvy investments in the stock market will neither make you ineligible for benefits nor result in a benefit cut. There is, however, an exception to this rule. If you continue to work while receiving Social Security, and your earnings exceed an annual limit, your benefits may be cut. (See below for an explanation of the earnings limit.)

HOW TO MAXIMIZE YOUR RETIREMENT BENEFIT*

Now that you know the basics of how Social Security works, let's see what you can do to make sure you receive the highest possible benefit.

*This section is adapted from an article by the author published in the July 1997 issue of *Money* magazine.

Disability and Survivors Benefits

In addition to your retirement benefit, there are two other types of Social Security payments you should be aware of: disability and survivor benefits.

You may receive a disability benefit if you have an injury or condition that impairs your ability to work and earn at least $500 per month for at least a year or is expected to result in your death. You can qualify for disability at any age, as long as you worked and paid Social Security taxes. (For more information on this topic, call the Social Security Administration toll-free line listed at the end of this chapter.)

Spouses are eligible for survivor's benefits based on a deceased spouse's working record. If you are widowed, you may begin to collect survivors benefits at age sixty; if you are disabled, at age fifty. (If you are widowed and caring for small children, you may be eligible for these benefits at a younger age. For more information, call the SSA toll-free line.)

Even if you are divorced, if your ex-spouse dies and had qualified for full Social Security benefits, you may be eligible for a widow or widower's benefit. To collect this benefit, however, you must have been married for at least ten years and either be currently unmarried or not have remarried until after you turned sixty, and you must not be entitled to a greater benefit on your own wage record. If you are widowed and remarry before you reach age sixty, you will not be able to collect benefits based on your former spouse's record. If you remarry after age sixty, you will qualify to receive whichever is higher—the benefit earned by either your former spouse or your current one.

In general, the more money you earn, the higher your Social Security benefit will be. However, there are limits on how high your benefit can rise.

One is the limit on the "maximum earnings taxable." This refers to the amount of your earnings on which your payroll or FICA tax is paid. In 2001, you must pay the tax on up to $80,400 of income. The amount increases slightly each year based on the national average wage. Once you earn the maximum in a particular year, you do not pay any more FICA tax for that year. But you also do not increase your future benefit. Even if you earn more than the maximum taxable amount for many years, you could not increase your benefit at all.

The second legal brake on your benefits is called the "earnings limit." This comes into play if you start to receive your Social Security benefit but continue to work. Once you have retired, and you earn wages over a certain dollar level, the Social Security system will dock your benefit until you reach age sixty-five.

In 2000, President Clinton signed a bill eliminating the earnings limit for people who are sixty-five or older. But younger Social Security beneficiaries still are subject to the limit. Here's how it works:

In 2001, for example, if you are under sixty-five, you will lose one of every two dollars of your benefit for every dollar you earn over $10,680. People who are on Social Security the year they turn sixty-five will also be subject to a limit, which is $25,000 in 2001. Their benefit will be cut by $1 for every $3 they earn above the limit. How can you guarantee that you'll receive the highest benefit, either now or in the future? Here are several strategies. One, or some combination of these, may work for you.

BEFORE YOU RETIRE

1. If you earn less than the maximum taxable earnings, consider moonlighting or developing a small business on the side.

The formula for calculating benefits averages your earnings over thirty-five years, assuming that you have worked at least that many years. If, as usually happens, you have the highest earnings toward the end of your career, you'll raise your benefit by working at a higher rate for as many years as possible.

If you do not make the maximum taxable earnings, consider boosting your income and your lifetime average by activities such as consulting; converting your woodworking hobby into a legitimate, profit-making business; or setting up a weekend catering operation. This strategy will help you most if you're in a career path that won't take your regular earnings to the maximum contribution level.

Don't assume that the tax hit on your added income will not be worth the extra work. With a sideline business profit of $10,000 a year added to your pre-tax income, you could still hike your annual average earnings—and your lifetime Social Security benefit base—by an average of several thousand dollars. If you're not sure how this would work for you, ask your accountant or other financial advisor to help you crunch the numbers.

2. Plan work force absences carefully.

When you're deciding whether to take time off to raise a child or care for an ailing relative, the impact of this decision on your retirement benefits may be the last thing in your mind. But you should consider it, because every year that you have zero earnings, work part-time, or earn less than your full salary, you are probably dragging your future retirement benefit down.

Women need to be especially vigilant about work force absences. That's because women's Social Security benefits average about 25 percent less than men's—not because of a gender difference written into the law, but because their work history tends to differ from men's. If you are thirty-five years old, for example, and decide to stay home for fifteen years while raising a family, you'll have fifteen zeroes in the computation of your annual earnings record. As a result, you may have to either settle for a lower benefit or work until you're older to come up with thirty-five years that will give you a better retirement payment.

WHEN YOU RETIRE

3. If you earn less than your spouse, or are not working for a salary, consider starting to take your benefit at age sixty-two.
If you'd like to boost the family income while you're still in your sixties, this strategy may help you. Let's look at an example: Nancy is sixty-two. The only time she worked outside the home was for ten years before she got married and had her children. If she retires now, she's entitled to a monthly payment of $400 (after the 20 percent reduction for retirement at age sixty-two). When Nancy's husband retires at age sixty-five, his monthly Social Security benefit will be $1,350. Nancy could retire today and receive the $400 per month, based on her own earnings. Then when her husband retires, she could receive a benefit based on his work record. This will come to $540, or half of his benefit ($675), reduced by 20 percent because she took early retirement.

4. Collect benefits based on the work record of your divorced spouse.
If your own earnings were sporadic or low, this entitlement—half of what your ex-spouse would collect at age sixty-five—could pay you a larger benefit than your own work history. You can start collecting this benefit as early as age sixty-two, even before your ex-spouse retires. And, what's more, your claim to the benefit will not affect the size of your ex's—in fact, he or she doesn't even have to know you're collecting it! To qualify, you need to meet the following criteria:
- You must have been married for at least ten years
- You cannot be married to someone else
- The benefit you'd receive based on your ex-spouse's work record must be larger than the benefit you'd receive based on your own work history
- If your ex has not signed up for Social Security yet, you must have been divorced for at least two years

If you are contemplating a divorce, don't forget the ten-year rule. If you've been married, say, nine years, and you have been earning less than your spouse, you may want to preserve your right to the divorce benefit by postponing the official break until you pass the ten-year mark. And, by the way, don't forget to keep a record of your spouse's Social Security number so that you can expedite your application for benefits.

5. Collect a benefit for your school-aged child.

You may think you can't afford to retire with a child still in school, but Uncle Sam can help out by providing a benefit for a child or children under age eighteen, or under nineteen for children who are still attending elementary or secondary school full-time.

You can take advantage of this rule if you had a child late in life or married someone who is younger or has younger children. Here's an example of how it works. Let's say that when you retire, you'll qualify for a monthly benefit of $1,200. If you do retire, you may collect an additional 50 percent, or $600, raising the total to $1,800 per month, for your sixteen-year-old. If you have two or more children still in school, you could get up to 88 percent more than your basic benefit.

6. Take advantage of the "special rule" exception to the earnings penalty.

As described above, if you earn more than the earnings limit—$10,680 if you are under age sixty-five, and $25,000 if you are between sixty-five and sixty-nine in 2001—you'll have your retirement benefit reduced according to a special formula. (There is no earnings limit once you reach full retirement age, which for people born before 1938 is sixty-five.) Here's how it works: Let's say you leave work in July at age sixty-two and seven months, after earning $40,000 from January through June, or $29,320 more than the limit of $10,680. Normally, your benefit would be reduced by one dollar for every two dollars you earned over the threshold, or $14,660— enough to likely prevent you from getting benefits for the entire year.

Because of this special one-time rule, however, in your first calendar year of retirement your earnings will be looked at on a monthly rather than a yearly basis. You may collect your full Social Security check in any month after you begin benefits, as long as your earnings after you retire don't exceed $890 a month (one-twelfth of the current earnings limit). So under this rule you could receive benefits for July through December as long as you did not have earnings over $890 in any of those months.

7. If you collect royalties, payments such as vacation or back pay, or sales commissions after you retire, this income may not be subject to the earnings limit. Be sure to tell Social Security about any "special payments" you may receive.

"Special payments" are income you receive for work completed before retirement. They include royalties from a book you wrote or a patent you secured before age sixty-five; benefits such as vacation, sick pay, and severance pay; and back pay and sales commissions. Common examples of special payments are commissions that insurance agents receive for policies sold before they retired, and income from the sale of agricultural crops that have been stored and are sold after the farmer retires.

As described earlier, your Social Security benefits may be reduced when you exceed certain income limits if you are less than seventy years old. But unless you know how the "special payments" rule works, your check may be reduced more than necessary.

Here are two examples of how this provision works:

• Barbara retired at age sixty-three from her job as an accountant. She started collecting Social Security but also continued to work for a few private clients. During her first year of retirement, she made $17,000 from that practice. Since this exceeds the $10,680 earnings limit, Social Security would have reduced her benefit according to the formula. Those earnings, however, consisted of $10,000 in fees and $7,000 for vacation and sick leave she had not used while on the job. Because the "special payment" of $7,000 could be subtracted from her earnings of $17,000, Barbara's earnings were in effect reduced to $10,000, so her benefit was not cut that year.

Stay Out of "Suspense"

Have you changed your name due to marriage or divorce? Have you used a nickname such as Maggie, instead of your full name, Margaret? Signed some of your employment records as Margaret Jones, M.D.? Spent a few summers working in a bar at the beach, or picking artichokes in California? People who change their name, use a nickname or a title, or work in service or agricultural businesses are most vulnerable to losing Social Security credit for their earnings.

How could this happen? When Social Security receives a W-2 or self-employment tax form with a name and Social Security number that don't match, the agency refers it to the "suspense file." After the reports are subjected to several manual and computerized processes, the yearly average of reports in the file is about 1.5 to 2 percent. If some of your earnings are in that file, you could receive a lower benefit than you deserve, or—if you can't prove that you've worked for the minimum of ten years required—you may not qualify for any benefit at all.

To make sure that your earnings don't end up in the suspense file, which contains $200 billion in earnings:

• Make sure that you are using exactly the same name on all of your employment records—that's the one on your Social Security card.

• If you change your name for any reason, report it to Social Security by calling the toll-free number.

• Read your Social Security Statement carefully. If you see a zero or lower income than should be there for a particular year, collect evidence of your employment—W-2 forms, tax forms, and the like—and call Social Security to arrange to have the missing earnings credited to your account.

Remember: You are probably the only person in the world who can get your earnings out of suspense—and the only one who cares enough to bother to do it.

Albert wrote a classic college textbook in 1980, and each year he receives royalty payments from the sales. In 1996, when he retired at age sixty-five, the royalty check was $14,000. Although Albert must report the income to Social Security, since the book was written before he retired none of his royalty payment is counted toward the earnings limit, and he will receive his full Social Security benefit.

DECISIONS YOU NEED TO MAKE ABOUT SOCIAL SECURITY

SHOULD YOU WORK FOR YOURSELF OR FOR AN EMPLOYER?

As downsizing, outsourcing, and part-time employment take their toll in industries that have traditionally relied on full-time, permanent employees, many people decide they would prefer to be self-employed. For Social Security purposes, the key difference between being employed and being your own boss is that if you work for yourself, you personally contribute twice as much of your earnings to Social Security through the FICA tax as you would if you had an employer.

Here's an illustration: Your employer, Apex Systems, Inc., withholds 7.65 percent of each paycheck (6.2 percent is for Social Security and the rest goes to Medicare) and sends it to the government. Apex Systems contributes an equal amount. However, if you become a full-time, self-employed computer consultant, you personally must pay the entire 15.3 percent— in effect, the shares of both employer and employee. In this case you must pay the Internal Revenue Service the 15.3 percent of your income on a quarterly basis along with your other esti-mated taxes. If your estimate was significantly below what you should have paid, you'll owe a penalty on April 15. Currently, the Internal Revenue Code provides some tax relief by allowing you to deduct one-half of the tax you paid on 92.35 percent of your self-employment earnings before calculating your taxable income.

Using Your Social Security Statement for Retirement Planning

Every American who is twenty-five or older and has worked at a job covered by Social Security at any time should now receive an annual Social Security statement about three months before his or her birthday. The statement, a four-page report on your Social Security status, is a crucial tool for planning your retirement.

If you are not receiving your Statement automatically, you can request it by calling Social Security's toll-free line, 1-800-772-1213, or by filling out a request form on the website, www.ssa.gov.

When you receive the statement, here is how you can use it for planning your retirement finances:

• Check the year-by-year "earnings record" to make sure that Social Security has a complete record of all your work credits. If this record is not complete, you could end up receiving a smaller benefit. If you see a year with a zero, or a number that is smaller than your earnings, contact your employer from that year to document your earnings. If you can't find the employer, call Social Security for help.

• Look at the section called "Your Estimated Benefits." Study the numbers that show the size of your benefit if you retire at different ages.

• If you use a computer, visit the Social Security website and use the figures on your statement to calculate the effect of retiring at different ages, with different income levels. You can do this by clicking on "Retirement Planners" on the SSA home page.

• If your Social Security benefit is going to be lower than you expected, see the section of this chapter starting on page 15 for tips on how to maximize your future benefit.

These facts seem to suggest that working for yourself puts you at a great financial disadvantage. Yet, with the uncertainties of the current job market, in some cases self-employment could actually provide you with a more stable income over the years and reduce your risk of going through extended periods of lay-offs or hunting for a new job.

But there are other considerations. For example, the amount of cash that you must pay in self-employment tax four times a year affects the size of your disposable income and savings. So perhaps you would be better off taking your risks in a company job, where the money that, if you were self-employed, would go to FICA, could instead be placed in a 401(k) account, an IRA, or other retirement investment, or could be used to pay off your home mortgage.

The decision about whether to work for someone else or for yourself must be based on many factors, including personal as well as financial considerations. What's important is that when you consider the financial impact of these options, you are aware of the effects that different FICA contributions may have on your current lifestyle.

WHEN SHOULD YOU RETIRE?

Your age as well as the month of the year in which you start receiving Social Security benefits may make a significant difference in the amount you receive. You have several options:

"Full Retirement Age"

This is the age when you receive what is generally referred to as your full or normal benefit. That age is sixty-five for people born in 1937 or earlier. For people who were born between 1938 and 1960, that age will rise according to the schedule shown in Chart 1-A (p. 24). By 2027, full retirement age will be sixty-seven for people born after 1959.

Early Retirement, Age Sixty-Two to Sixty-Five

As we have seen, you can start collecting Social Security as early as age sixty-two, but will receive a permanently lower benefit if

Chart 1-A

Full Retirement Age, Based on Year of Birth	
Year of Birth	**Full Retirement Age**
1937 or earlier	65
1938	65 and 2 months
1939	65 and 4 months
1940	65 and 6 months
1941	65 and 8 months
1942	65 and 10 months
1943-1954	66
1955	66 and 2 months
1956	66 and 4 months
1957	66 and 6 months
1958	66 and 8 months
1959	66 and 10 months
1960 and later	67

you do that rather than waiting until full retirement age, which is currently sixty-five.

If you retire between age sixty-two and the current full retirement age of sixty-five, your benefit will be reduced between 20 percent and ⅚ of one percent (if you retire one month before turning sixty-five). The longer you wait, the less the reduction will be. (Chart 1-B illustrates how the reduced benefits are phased in.)

Who should retire early? Bruce Schobel, a former Social Security Administration actuary who is now a vice president at New York Life Insurance Co. in New York City, says that in making this decision you should be sure to consider "any special knowledge you have about your mortality." If members of your family tend to live well into their nineties, "you would be well advised to wait until age sixty-five, because the 20 percent reduction in benefit starting at age sixty-two will be too great for you," especially if your other resources will dwindle in later life. Conversely, if you have, for example, a heart problem that your doctor says places you at high risk, start collecting benefits as soon as you are eligible to do so.

Delayed Retirement, Age Sixty-Five to Seventy
If you want to keep working full-time, you can postpone taking your benefit and, ultimately, increase it. Under current law, your payment could go up as little as 3 percent, for people who were born in 1917 through 1924, and as much as 8 percent, if

Chart 1-B

Percentage of Full Benefits You Will Receive if You Were Born in 1937 or Earlier and You Retire Before Age 65	
64½	96⅔%
64	93⅓%
63½	90%
63	86⅔%
62½	83⅓%
62	80%

you were born in 1943 or after. (Chart 1-C illustrates how much you can increase your benefit by delaying your retirement.)

Like most government policies that are subject to change if Congress decides to amend the law, these rules are not written in stone. Some experts have suggested that one way to decrease the flow of funds from the Social Security system would be to raise the full retirement age at a faster pace. For example, a person born in 1940 might end up receiving full retirement benefits at age sixty-seven, not at age sixty-six and six months as the current law provides.

Chart 1-C

How Much You Can Increase Your Benefit by Postponing Signing Up for Social Security Until You Are Up to 70 Years Old.	
Year of Birth	**Yearly Rate of Increase**
1917-1924	3%
1925-1926	3.5%
1927-1928	4%
1929-1930	4.5%
1931-1932	5%
1933-1934	5.5%
1935-1936	6%
1937-1938	7%
1939-1940	7.5%
1941-1942	7.5%
1943 or later	8%

Careful Selection of Your Retirement Month

Be mindful of the month, as well as the year, that you choose to retire. Your choice could mean the gain or loss of several thousand dollars in the course of that year. Here's an example that explains why:

Sandra sells women's clothing in a neighborhood shop. She will turn sixty-five in July 2001. Between January and June 2001, she will receive a salary of $13,400. If Sandra retires in July, her income for the year will be:

$13,400 in salary, January through June 2001
$ 6,000 based on $1,000 per month in Social Security for July 2001 through December 2001
_____
$19,400 total for 2001

For Sandra, waiting until June to sign up for Social Security benefits could be a costly mistake. Here's why:

The law says that if you earn $25,000 or less (in 2001; this changes annually) from working in the year you reach full retirement age (currently age 65) you may take early retirement and receive reduced Social Security benefits for all twelve months of the year. So if Sandra starts to collect her Social Security benefit early, in January, and continues to work on her job until June, she will receive approximately 97 percent of her benefit—$972 per month for an additional six months. Then her income for 2001 will become:

$ 5,832 for Social Security benefits, January through June
$13,400 for her salary through June
$ 5,832 for Social Security benefits, July through December
_____
$25,064 total

This is $5,664 more than if Sandra went on Social Security in July.

Make a Date With Social Security

Talk with a Social Security representative—either by calling the toll-free number or by visiting your local office—six months to a year before you intend to retire. The representative can help you calculate the impact of various retirement dates on the size of your future benefit. Be sure to go to Social Security to file your claim at least six months before the date you select.

You can find the address of the closest Social Security office through the toll-free information line or from your local phone book

---

Some caveats: Taking early retirement reduces your monthly benefit *forever*. It will never go up to the full amount after that first year. The benefit is actually reduced ⅝ of one percent for each month early that you retire. You'll also want to assess the income tax implications of this decision.

Should you tap all of your retirement income at the same time? Hopefully, Social Security will not be the only income you rely on in retirement. If you have access to a private pension or to tax-deferred retirement savings plans, their rules may differ from Social Security's. For example, you may start withdrawing money from an Individual Retirement Account at age fifty-nine and a half without penalty, and you will be penalized if you do not start to withdraw it at age seventy and a half (see Chapter Three).

Another example: if you want to stop working at sixty-two, but will receive enough money to live on from your pension or savings, you may want to postpone collecting Social Security until you are sixty-five or even seventy and thus receive a greater benefit.

Before setting a date for full or partial retirement, be sure to review all of your potential income sources so that you can orchestrate collection of your retirement income from various sources in the most favorable way.

THE TAX FACTOR

What Uncle Sam gives, he may also take away. The relationship between Social Security and taxes is a good example of this maxim. You pay a percentage of your earnings into the Social Security system. Uncle Sam returns some (actually, in most cases, much more) of what you contributed in the form of a retirement benefit. Then he takes back some of it in income taxes on your Social Security.

The pre-retirement relationship between taxes and Social Security is very straightforward. Before you retire, you pay a Social Security and Medicare tax on your income of either 15.3 percent, if you are self-employed, or 7.65 percent, if you work for an employer.

Once you have retired, if your income from all sources exceeds certain limits, you must pay some taxes on your Social Security benefits.

To figure out whether you must pay taxes on your Social Security benefit, add up the year's income from wages, salaries, and tax-exempt, and even non-tax-exempt, interest and dividends. If it comes to less than $25,000 for an individual and $32,000 for a couple, you will not have to pay federal taxes. About 80 percent of retirees fall into this category.

However, if the income is between $25,000 and $34,000 for an individual or $32,000 to $44,000 for a couple, you must pay an income tax on 50 percent of your Social Security benefits. If the income is higher, you must pay tax on 85 percent of it. The percentage of your benefit that is subject to the tax is added to your other income, and the tax is computed on the total adjusted gross income.

For example, Andrew earned $20,000 from non-Social Security sources and $14,000 from his Social Security last year, for a total of $34,000. He must pay taxes on half, or $7,000, of the Social Security benefits income, because the total was between $25,000 and $34,000.

* * *

Mastering the nuances of how Social Security works can be a daunting task. That's because the current program has evolved from more than sixty years of negotiated, political compromises by Congress, the White House, and interest groups that are active in the lobbying process.

• Still, you should not minimize or ignore the importance of Social Security to your future just because it is complicated.

• Social Security is the one source of retirement income that is accessible to virtually every American.

• For most of us, Social Security is the only retirement income that comes with a built-in cost-of-living increase.

• You do not have to be a stock market whiz or a fanatical saver to qualify or to benefit. All you have to do to get it is be a good citizen: work and pay your rightful taxes.

FOR MORE INFORMATION

BY TELEPHONE

Internal Revenue Service
For information on tax treatment of Social Security benefits, order Publication 915, "Social Security and Equivalent Railroad Retirement Benefits," from the toll-free publications line, 1-800-829-3676.

National Committee to Preserve Social Security and Medicare (NCPSSM)
This organization of 5.5 million members lobbies in Washington on behalf of Social Security supporters. You can get answers to general Social Security questions, help with a problem with your own

benefit or account, and written information on issues such as cost-of-living increases, by calling their toll-free line, 1-800-966-1935.

Older Women's League (OWL)

"The voice of mid-life and older women," OWL has chapters nationwide. To locate the one nearest you, or for a list of OWL's publications on income security and other issues, call 1-800-825-3695.

Social Security Administration (SSA)

You can call the toll-free line, 1-800-772-1213 (TDD 1-800-325-0778). Operators answer the phone on business days between 7 A.M. and 7 P.M., but automated messages will help you with certain requests—such as ordering your Social Security Statement—24 hours a day. Phone lines are busiest early in the week and early in the month. Services available through this line include correcting errors in your Statement, locating the Social Security office closest to you, and ordering

---

Staying Current on Social Security

The Social Security Administration's toll-free fax line, 1-888-475-7000, can provide a wealth of information about how the program works.

However, many of the fact sheets available through this line contain outdated figures that are important in calculating your potential Social Security benefits or taxes. By all means, order the information available through the fax, but be sure to check the date on the fact sheet. If the date is not in the current year, you need to call the SSA toll-free information line, 1-800-772-1213, and ask a customer service representative for the most current data.

some publications. For an overview of SSA's programs, request a free copy of "Social Security: Understanding The Benefits" (Pub. No. 05-10024). More detailed free publications include "Social Security: What You Need To Know When You Get Retirement or Survivors Benefits," (No. 05-10077) and "Social Security: What Every Woman Should Know" (No. 05-10127).

The SSA maintains 1,300 field offices around the country. To find the location and number of an office close to you, call the national toll-free line. Some SSA offices will allow you to make an appointment by calling ahead and others will insist that you drop in and wait your turn. If you have access to a fax, dial the SSA toll-free line, 1-888-475-7000, for instructions on how to order a wide range of free fact sheets.

Women's Institute for a Secure Retirement (WISER)
To order copies of a useful pamphlet, "What Every Woman Needs to Know About Money and Retirement," call this non-profit organization, whose goal is to educate women about financial security issues, at 202-343-5452.

BY MAIL

SSA
Because information is so readily available through the agency's toll-free phone and fax lines as well as through the Internet, you probably shouldn't bother to send a written request. However, if you want to do so, the address is: SSA, Office of Public Inquiries, 6401 Security Blvd., Room 4-C-5 Annex, Baltimore, MD 21235. See "By telephone," above, for names of some free publications.

Women's Institute for a Secure Retirement (WISER)
You may order a fifteen-page pamphlet, "What Every Woman Needs to Know About Money and Retirement," by writing to WISER at 1201 Pennsylvania Ave. N.W., Suite 619, Washington, DC 20004 and enclosing three dollars for shipping and handling.

ON THE INTERNET

www.ncpssm.org

At the site of the National Committee to Preserve Social Security and Medicare you can keep up with current legislation and other news about Social Security and Medicare.

www.ssa.gov

The SSA website provides extensive information about how the program works, answers to frequently asked questions, and the text of many publications. To pose questions about SSA publications and public information, or leave comments and suggestions about Social Security Online—but not to request information about your personal situation—you may send a message to the following e-mail address: webmaster@ssa.gov.

CHAPTER TWO

Your Pension Plan

A U.S. Department of Labor press release announced the following news:

> A former New York City woman, now living in Richmond, VA, pleaded guilty Thursday to embezzling $563,762 from the employee retirement fund of George B. Buck Consulting Actuaries, Inc., headquartered in New York City.
>
> In her role as the payroll manager of . . . (the) employee benefit consulting firm, Donna Moreno fraudulently prepared approximately 226 pension checks made out to deceased and former participants of the plan. She cashed the checks against the company's petty cash fund, which she also controlled.

A federal court ordered Moreno to pay back the money she embezzled, spend weekends in prison for a year, serve five years on probation, and perform community service. The Labor Department, which brought the lawsuit, says that Moreno was sentenced (only) to weekends in jail because she was the sole caregiver for an aged mother.

This case holds a particular irony: The criminal who stole from an employee pension fund worked for a company that advises other companies on how to manage their pension funds!

The great majority of the more than $3 trillion that is held for Americans in pension savings is managed legally, so you can count on collecting your rightful share when you retire. On the other hand, the Buck Consulting case is not unique. In

November 1995, the Labor Department launched a campaign to root out pension fraud, a campaign which included the installation of a toll-free hotline through which people could report suspicions of illegal activity. By the end of 2000, the Department had recovered more than $100 million for workers whose pension savings had been misused, and closed more than 2,600 investigations that resulted in violations and recovery of funds.

Do you know what pension savings you are entitled to? Do you know if your pension savings are secure? How can you tell? How do federal laws protect your pension, and what do you need to know to be sure that the laws are being followed?

This chapter describes the role of the federal government in overseeing most pension funds that are held in trust for you by your employer. If you own or work for a small business, are self-employed, or want information about supplementing your pension with additional retirement savings, see Chapter Three for information about the new SIMPLE plan for small business, Simplified Employee Pensions (SEPs), Keogh Plans, and Individual Retirement Accounts.

WHAT YOU NEED TO KNOW ABOUT PENSION PLANS

About half of American workers are covered by some type of pension or retirement savings plan in their current job. According to the Employee Benefits Research Institute, in 1998, this was 44 percent of women and 50 percent of employed men. How much money you get, when you get it, and in what form you get it depends on the amount and management of contributions by your employer or yourself, plus the earnings from investing these savings.

Behind the scenes, however, stands another big player who influences the type and the size of the pension you receive: Uncle Sam. Your employer holds your pension savings in trust for you until you retire. But it's Uncle Sam you must rely on to make sure that all the money you're entitled to is really available, and that your employer has not misused it, deceived you, or, as a side effect of going bankrupt, cheated you out of your pension.

If you're not a pension lawyer or employee benefits professional, you certainly don't need to know all the details of the complex federal role in overseeing your pension. But to make sure that you and your family will be protected in retirement, you should learn the basics of your own plan and know exactly what your rights are if you suspect that the plan is not being managed properly.

Most pension plans must comply with government rules based on the Employee Retirement Income Security Act of 1974, known as ERISA, and amendments to that law. These rules govern how much money you or your employer may contribute to your pension plan, when and how you may collect your pension, how the money is invested, and what information the company must give you about how the plan operates. An employer who breaks these rules is subject to penalties, including fines and jail sentences. Unless otherwise noted, the nine following key points apply to plans that are subject to ERISA.

But note—the ERISA protections described in this section do not apply to the following types of pension plans:

• Federal, state, or local government pension plans, including plans of certain international organizations

• Certain church or church association plans

• Plans maintained solely to comply with state workers' compensation, unemployment compensation, or disability insurance laws

• Unfunded excess benefit plans—those maintained solely to provide benefits or contributions in excess of those allowed for most retirement plans

1. THERE ARE TWO MAIN TYPES OF PENSIONS PLANS OFFERED BY EMPLOYERS: DEFINED BENEFIT PLANS AND DEFINED CONTRIBUTION PLANS.

A *defined benefit plan* offers what most of us consider the traditional pension: a guarantee that when you retire, your employer will pay you a certain sum for life—say, $300 per month—

based on a formula that typically includes how many years you've worked in your job and your salary at the time you retire. In this type of plan, the company establishes a fund used to pay employees' pensions. You do not have an "account" in your own name, and your employer or other plan administrator—not you—makes decisions on how to invest the money in the pension fund. The company is obligated to pay you the promised benefit, even if the pension fund's investments do not perform as well as expected.

A *defined contribution* plan is just what it sounds like: a plan to which you, and sometimes your employer, contribute a certain amount of money, usually on a regular basis, to a retirement account in your name. This type of plan does *not* guarantee you a fixed amount of money when you retire. When you stop working, you may have a choice of whether to take your benefit in a lump sum or in an annuity payment that you receive on a regular basis, such as once a month, over a period of years or for your lifetime.

There are different types of defined contribution plans, each with its own rules. Your employer decides which types of plan or plans to offer. Most, but not all, employers also offer several investment options—such as mutual funds, your company's stock, or a government bond fund—to choose from for your account. The amount you may contribute to the pension plan, and the investment earnings you reap from it, depend on two factors—federal law and the options your employer chooses to offer you.

2. THE MOST COMMON TYPE OF DEFINED CONTRIBUTION PLAN IS CALLED A 401(K).

A 401(k) is named after the section of the Internal Revenue Code that authorizes this type of plan. Technically, a 401(k) is a "salary deferral" plan, because the money you contribute actually comes from your salary. The money you save in a 401(k) can come from these sources:

Employee Tax-Deductible Contribution
Each year you may contribute a portion of your salary up to a limit set by the Internal Revenue Service, adjusted annually for inflation. In 2001, the limit is $10,500.

Employee After-Tax Contribution
If your plan allows it, you may contribute additional money, on which you'll have to pay regular income tax. However, you won't have to pay income tax on the earnings from these funds until you withdraw them from the 401(k).

Employer Matching Contribution
Your employer may choose to "match" some of the money you put into your 401(k). A 1999 study by Hewitt Associates benefits consultants found that in 1999, 92 percent of those companies contributed matching funds to employees' accounts, and most of them limited the contribution to seven percent or less of the employee's annual salary.

The exact amounts that you and your employer may put into your 401(k) each year can vary, depending on what the plan must do to meet IRS requirements designed to prevent your plan from becoming a retirement vehicle that benefits primarily the company's executives rather than employees. If you have a defined contribution plan, the total pre- and after-tax contributions you may make in 1999 is 25 percent of your salary or $30,000 in one year, except for 401(k) plans, which have a limit of $10,500. For a defined benefit plan, the limit is 100 percent of your salary or $140,000, whichever is less.

3. THE AMOUNT OF THE PENSION YOU RECEIVE WHEN YOU RETIRE DEPENDS ON SEVERAL FACTORS.
In a *defined benefit* plan, the amount you receive depends on your employer's formula, usually based on your years of service and your salary at the time you retire. In most *defined contribution plans,* however, you personally may play a major role in

An Array of Defined Contribution Plans

Each type of defined contribution plan regulated by the federal government has its own rules on issues such as how much you can contribute, when you can receive the money, and taxes you must pay on withdrawals. If you have one of these plans, you should carefully read the Summary Plan Document available from the plan administrator so that you know what the rules are.

In addition to 401(k) plans, the most common types of defined contribution plans include:

403(b): Tax-deferred annuities or pensions provided by certain schools, colleges, and other non-profit organizations.

Sec. 457: Similar to a 401(k) deferred compensation plan for employees of state and local government.

Employee Stock Ownership Plans (ESOPs): Assets in the plan must consist primarily of company stock, at least 51 percent.

Money Purchase Plan: Employer makes a fixed contribution, money cannot be withdrawn before the employee leaves the job or retires.

Profit Sharing or Stock Bonus: Employer decides each year whether and how much to contribute to the plan, which allocates the amount to employees by formula out of profits or other company funds. After 401(k)s, this is the most widely available type of defined contribution plan.

Thrift Plan: A type of profit-sharing plan to which employees may contribute after-tax money. Contributions may or may not be matched by the employer.

determining the size of your pension. That's because it's usually up to you to make two key decisions: how much money to put into the account, and how to invest the money. (In some cases, an employer may use a managed trust to invest the funds for you.) The Labor Department encourages companies to provide you with "investor education" information to help you understand the pros and cons of the choices. But the exact number and type of investments offered is totally up to your employer.

4. YOU HAVE A LEGAL RIGHT TO THE MONEY YOU PERSONALLY CONTRIBUTE TO YOUR DEFINED CONTRIBUTION PLAN AT ANYTIME.

However, to collect what your employer has contributed, and the earnings on your pension fund investments, you must be "vested," meaning that you have worked for your employer for a certain number of years.

And if you take money out of your defined contribution plan before you turn fifty-nine and a half, in most cases you'll have to pay a penalty tax of 10 percent on that amount, as well as the income tax.

5. BOTH THE FEDERAL GOVERNMENT AND YOUR OWN PENSION PLAN HAVE RULES THAT DETERMINE WHEN YOU CAN START TO COLLECT YOUR PENSION.

Your retirement plan should specify the age at which you are eligible to receive your pension. If you leave your job before that age—unless there are special circumstances, such as a disability—you may forfeit some of the pension you expected to receive. Some plans specify an "early retirement" age, such as fifty-five or fifty-eight, at which you can receive a pension, but the benefit will be lower than if you wait until full retirement age.

Your employer may not capriciously postpone giving you your pension when you have earned it. ERISA requires your employer to begin payment by the sixtieth day after the end of the plan year (the fiscal year, which may be different from the calendar year) in which the *latest* of the following events occurs:

How Long Before I'm Vested?

If you don't know the answer to this question, look it up in the Summary Plan Document you should have received within ninety days of enrolling in the plan. If you have a defined benefit plan, you will not have access to any of your pension benefit until you are vested. If you have a defined contribution plan you always have a right to the money *you* have contributed and the earnings on it when you leave the company—although you could pay a penalty for early withdrawal. But you do not have a right to any *employer's* contribution until you're vested.

ERISA allows employers to select one of the following sets of minimum standards for vesting:

Seven-year Graded Vesting Schedule
To qualify under this system, you must work for your employer for at least three years. For each year between your third and seventh, you vest an additional 20 percent of your accrued pension benefit. Thus, if you retire after four years and before five, you'll get 40 percent of the accrued benefit. If you work for seven years, you'll get 100 percent.

Five-year "Cliff" Vesting
In this system, none of your accrued benefit is vested until you have worked five years. After five years, you are 100 percent vested.

Remember that these are minimum standards—some companies set a shorter period for vesting.

- You reach sixty-five or, if it is earlier, the normal retirement age specified by your plan;
- The end of the tenth year after you began participating in the plan; or
- You stop working for the employer.

6. YOUR SPOUSE OR EX-SPOUSE MAY BE ENTITLED TO
BENEFITS FROM YOUR PENSION PLAN.

If you get a divorce, you may be entitled to benefits from your spouse's pension plan, either before or after your spouse's retirement or death. To gain access to these benefits, you must have an agreement that meets the specific legal requirements of a document called a Qualified Domestic Relations Order (QDRO). You should get expert legal advice on this issue if it applies to you.

If you are married, both ERISA and your own pension plan contain rules specifying whether your spouse can receive benefits from your pension plan if you die. Different rules apply, depending on whether you die before starting to collect the pension or afterwards; and depending on which type of pension plan you have.

Defined Benefit Plan

If you participate in a *defined benefit* plan, your employer may offer your pension in the form of a life annuity or a lump sum. If you choose an annuity, you'll get regular payments once a month for a certain number of years, or for your lifetime. As long as you receive the pension, you would have rights under the plan—for example, you could receive a cost-of-living increase if the company decides to offer one.

If you take your pension as a lump sum, you should receive it in one—or possibly two or three—payments soon after you retire. Once you receive the payment, you no longer have any rights—such as entitlement to a cost of living increase—to benefits your employer may offer under the plan.

When you enroll in a pension plan, if you are married, ERISA requires your spouse to be the beneficiary of your

Cash Balance Plans

In recent years, numerous companies have created a new type of retirement account called a cash balance plan. In contrast to a traditional pension plan, which guarantees you a specific retirement benefit based on a formula, a cash balance plan does not guarantee you a pension of a specific amount.

Each employer sets the rules for a company's cash balance plan, but the amount that accrues in an account is based on two factors: An annual employer contribution equal to a flat percentage of your salary; and an "interest credit"—for example, the interest on a Treasury Bill plus one percent. Many employees whose companies have replaced other pension plans with cash balance plans claim that the new plans discriminate against mid-career and/or older workers. In many cases, they have demonstrated that such workers will end up receiving a lower pension than under the employer's previous system.

The Equal Employment Opportunity Commission, the federal agency that enforces the Age Discrimination in Employment Act, created a "team to study whether these plans are discriminatory," but at press time there had been no official ruling. For current information on cash balance plans, order the Labor Department's publication, "Cash Balance Plans: Questions and Answers," from the toll-free line, 1-800-998-7542, or read it on the website, at www.dol.gov/dol/pwba/pubs/cashbq&a.htm. Another resource is a website set up by employees who are protesting against the plans: www.cashpensions.com.

pension if you die, unless you both sign a waiver and another beneficiary is named. Specifically, your spouse will be entitled to a Qualified Preretirement Survivor Annuity (QPSA) and a Qualified Joint and Survivor Annuity (QJSA). The QPSA is the pension your spouse would receive if you died *before* you reached the minimum retirement age. A QJSA is the pension your spouse would receive if you died *after* you started receiving payment. In either case, the surviving spouse must receive at least 50 percent, and not more than 100 percent, of the benefit that the deceased spouse had been receiving.

The only way to divert your pension benefit from your husband or wife in the event of your death, is for both of you to sign a document called a waiver, giving up the spouse's right to his or her share of the pension. If you decide to sign the waiver, you may name another person, such as one of your children, to receive the pension. When your spouse signs the waiver, this is referred to as "spousal consent." To make the waiver legal, you must follow very specific requirements, including having the document signed by either a notary or an official of your pension plan. Make sure that you follow all of the steps in the procedure properly.

Your employer must provide you with general information about the terms of the QPSA and QJSA the company offers when you go to work for the company or reach age thirty-five, and again shortly before you retire. If your employer does not provide it, or if the explanation is not clear, you may request a specific description of your benefits and your employer must respond to you in writing within thirty days.

The dollar amount and type of benefits your spouse may receive from your pension if you die vary according to when you die, how long you have worked for your employer, what benefits you have earned, and the provisions of your pension plan.

Defined Contribution Plan

Most 401(k), profit-sharing, or similar plans require spousal consent for a withdrawal. However, some plans do specify that

What Women Need to Know and Do About Pensions

While all workers need to save more for retirement, women face additional challenges because they have lower earnings, experience higher job turnover, and are more often employed in industries with low or no pension coverage. Here's a list of questions women need to ask themselves about pensions (compiled by the Pension and Welfare Benefits Administration of the Labor Department):

- Does your employer have a pension plan?
- Do you know what type of plan it is?
- Are you included in the plan?
- Have you worked long enough to earn a pension?
- Do you know how much your pension will be?
- Do you know what happens to your pension if you retire early?
- Do you know what happens to a pension if you or your spouse dies?
- Is your pension insured?
- Do you have pension information from all your jobs?
- Do you know what benefits your spouse's plan provides?
- Are you entitled to a portion of your spouse's pension benefit if you get divorced?
- Do you know the Social Security benefits to which you are entitled?
- Can your pension benefits be reduced by Social Security or other government payments?
- Do you know how you can save for retirement if you do not have a pension plan?

a married employee's spouse is the beneficiary if the employee dies while employed.

When you are ready to start receiving an annuity or withdraw funds from most 401(k), profit sharing, or similar plans, you may be able to choose what type of payment you want to receive without your spouse's consent. If you select a life annuity, your spouse will automatically become the beneficiary in case of your death—unless you both sign a waiver under the QSJA rules described above. If you choose some other form of payout, such as a lump sum, your spouse's consent may be required, and your spouse does not automatically become the beneficiary. Some members of Congress have sponsored bills that would require spousal consent for a married person to take money out of a 401(k) at anytime, but they have not passed.

If you die before the date you would become eligible for your annuity or payout, your spouse will automatically receive the benefits—again, unless you have both waived them under the rules.

7. FEDERAL LAW REQUIRES YOUR EMPLOYER TO MEET CERTAIN STANDARDS FOR MANAGING AND INVESTING YOUR MONEY.

The money in your pension fund may be crucially important to your future. Yet, until you retire, that money is kept in a trust controlled, but not owned, by your employer or a plan manager hired by your employer. Here's what your employer must do to comply with the law, accompanied by some true stories of how those rules have been broken in the past. All of the lawsuits described in these examples were brought by the Labor Department.

Employers must keep the money in a trust, where it is not available to claims of the employer's creditors and not owned by the employee.

The owner of a bankrupt consulting firm in Vienna, VA, was charged with diverting employee contributions and failing to deposit employer matching funds to a 401(k). The person

Ten Warning Signs of 401(k) Abuse

The following list was issued by the Department of Labor. If you see any of these warning signs in your own plan, you should ask the plan administrator to explain them. If the explanation does not satisfy you, call the Department's Office of Technical Assistance, 202-219-8776, for information about what to do.

1. Your 401(k) statement is consistently late or comes at irregular intervals.

2. Your 401(k) account balance doesn't appear to be accurate.

3. Your employer held your contribution for more than ninety days.

4. There is a significant drop in your account balance that can't be explained by normal market ups-and-downs.

5. Your 401(k) statement shows your contribution from your paycheck wasn't made.

6. Investments listed in your account statement aren't the ones you authorized.

7. Former employees are having trouble getting their benefits paid on time or in correct amounts.

8. There have been unusual transactions, such as a loan to the employer, a corporate officer, or one of the plan trustees.

9. There have been frequent and unexplained changes in investment managers or consultants.

10. Your employer has recently experienced severe financial difficulty.

also allegedly mingled the retirement savings funds with other assets of the business.

Employers must invest the money in the employees' interest, as opposed to the interest of someone else.
The owner of a Philadelphia heating and air conditioning company pleaded guilty to using his employees' 401(k) assets for his own business, including taking "loans" from those accounts that he did not pay back. As a result, a federal court has ordered him to repay thousands of dollars to the plan, and when this book was published, he was awaiting criminal sentencing for embezzlement.

(A general exception to this rule is that your employer may invest up to 10 percent of your pension plan's money in your company's stock or in real estate leased to the employer. In certain cases—including profit sharing and employee stock ownership plans—the legal limit for this type of investment may be greater than 10 percent.)

Employers must limit expenses for managing the pension fund to those that are "reasonable."
A few years ago, the New York District Council of Carpenters was sued for, among other things, spending pension fund money on luxury vehicles equipped with cellular telephones, without determining whether they were needed and the costs were reasonable. An agreement between the union and the government requires union officials to keep detailed records showing that the vehicles and phones are actually used and necessary for pension fund business.

Employers must diversify the fund's investments.
A federal court found this rule had been broken in the case of a Las Vegas pension plan, whose trustees were found to have invested most of the fund in one real estate venture.

Employers must invest your money wisely and carefully.
Officials of an Alexandria, VA, firm offered employees the option of investing in Guaranteed Insurance Contracts (GICs)

sold by a company that went bankrupt. Company officials were found guilty of failing to "evaluate the financial stability, creditworthiness, and claims-paying ability" or to monitor the investments. The court ordered the officials to repay at least $525,000 to the employees who lost money.

8. YOU HAVE A RIGHT TO INFORMATION ABOUT YOUR PENSION BENEFITS, HOW TO COLLECT THEM, AND HOW YOUR PENSION PLAN IS BEING MANAGED.

Summary Plan Description (SPD)

Within ninety days of joining a pension plan, you should receive a Summary Plan Description (SPD) that provides basic information about who is responsible for your plan and how it works, including how you become eligible for your pension and how it is calculated. Read it, and if you don't understand anything in the SPD, ask your plan administrator to explain it.

As a plan participant, you should receive an SPD automatically every five years if there is a change, and every ten years if the plan is not changed. ERISA also requires your employer to provide you with an SPD at anytime if you make a request for it, although you may be charged a "reasonable fee" for the copy.

Summary Annual Report (SAR)

ERISA also requires pension plans to file more detailed reports that may offer clues to whether your plan is being properly managed. If you want to stay up to date on your plan's financial status, ask your plan administrator for a copy of the Summary Annual Report (SAR), a brief form of the much longer, more detailed report known as the Form 5500. The SAR contains information on your plan's expenses, the value of its assets (including whether the value has gone up or down), and in the case of a defined benefit plan, an actuary's statement as to whether your plan's assets are adequate to meet ERISA's requirements.

Form 5500

If the SAR does not answer all of your questions, you may

request a copy of the complete Form 5500 from your plan administrator. This form gives you more detailed information on how the plan has invested your money, how each investment has done during the year, and whether the plan has made loans or changed management frequently. For a large company, the Form 5500 plan can be voluminous. The Motorola, Inc., 1994 report on the company's savings and profit sharing plan, for example, numbered more than eighty pages.

Your plan administrator is required to give you a copy of the Form 5500, although you may be charged for photocopying. If the administrator doesn't give you a copy, and the reason for the delay is within his or her control, you may go to court to seek a fine of up to $110 per day for the period of delay.

9. ERISA RULES CONTROL YOUR PENSION RIGHTS IF YOUR PLAN IS TERMINATED OR YOUR COMPANY MERGES WITH ANOTHER COMPANY.

If your employer decides to close down the company, or a plant or division of the company, all of the benefits you have earned in your retirement account are vested as soon as the plan is terminated. If you have a defined benefit plan, your pension is protected by the Pension Benefit Guaranty Corporation (PBGC; see box on page 56). If your savings are in a defined contribution account, however, there is no federal guarantee.

Special Benefit for Defined Benefit Plan Pensions
The purchase of the Del Monte Corp. by a group of investors in a leveraged buyout posed a $90 million threat to the pension benefits of 6,700 workers and retirees in eight states.

According to the PBGC, a federal corporation, Del Monte's pension fund's assets were $260 million; its liabilities, $350 million. When PBGC became aware of the shortfall, it negotiated a deal requiring the company to contribute $55 million in cash to the fund over five years to secure the workers' benefits.

If you participate in a defined benefit plan, your pension has special protection from a federal insurance program operated by the PBGC. Unfortunately, PBGC's authority does not extend to

Questions to Ask About Your Employer's Pension Plan

1. Who is responsible for contributing to the plan—you, your employer, or both?

2. Is the plan insured by the Pension Benefit Guaranty Corporation?

3. What are the plan's eligibility rules?

4. How long must I participate to become vested?

5. Will my employer match my contributions and if so, how much will the company contribute?

6. Does the size of my benefits from the plan depend on investment performance?

7. Will I personally be responsible for investing the assets in my account? If the answer is yes, then ask:

- What investments alternatives are available?
- How often can I adjust investment decisions?
- What educational programs are available to help me make informed decisions?

8. Is the plan invested primarily in stock in my employer's company? If so, then ask yourself:

- What do I know about the financial condition of the company, and where can I get more information?
- Is the employer's stock publicly traded, which allows me to monitor it easily?
- If the stock is not publicly traded, how can I tell what it is worth? (And how often?)
- Under what circumstances am I allowed to diversify my investments?

defined contribution plans such as the 401(k).

Here's what PBGC does to prevent pension plan failures and guarantee workers' benefits:

• It operates an "early warning" system, monitoring more than four hundred underfunded plans, and intervenes—as in the Del Monte case—to prevent employees from actually losing their benefits;

• It monitors plans that close down, whether due to financial problems or simply because the company terminates them. In these cases, if the plan does not have enough money to pay all of the benefits, PBGC may take over the plan and pay out the benefits; and

• It guarantees the benefits of retirees and future retirees up to a level of $3,392.05 per month in 2001, for retirees sixty-five and over, and lesser amounts, on a sliding scale, for younger retirees. However, the amount of the pension you receive in these cases could be less than you expected.

Does your company's pension plan have enough money to pay all the benefits you're entitled to? How can you tell?

Each year, as required by ERISA, PBGC requires employers of about four million people in four thousand companies to send their employees a letter advising them that their defined benefit pension fund is funded at 90 percent or less than it needs to meet its obligations. When people receive these letters, says Judith Welles, director of communications and public affairs for PBGC, they "should not get shaken up." The letter "is an alert," she says, "a heads-up notice, but it doesn't mean there is going to be an immediate problem. However, that notice should tip you off to check on two key signals: the severity of your plan's underfunding, and the financial strength of the company you work for."

PBGC usually does not need to take over or reorganize a pension plan unless the funding goes below 60 percent, Welles says.

Until 1997, one way to find out if your company's pension plan had a serious problem was to consult PBGC's list of the fifty companies with the most seriously underfunded pension plans, updated and released annually in December. Since PBGC stopped publishing the list in response to employers' complaints, other sources you can tap for more details on the status of the plan and the company's financial health include:

• Your plan's Summary Annual Report (SAR), described on page 50, which summarizes the plan's financial status and must be available from your plan administrator within nine months of the end of the plan's fiscal year;

• Your plan's Summary of Material Modifications (SMM), a report on changes that have been made in plan rules that must be available within 210 days of the end of the plan's fiscal year; and

• If your company is publicly traded, annual reports that include basic financial data. (These reports do not include financial details of the pension funds, but may offer clues to the company's financial health.)

Because of the lag in the required time to file, information in the SAR and the SMM may not reflect the current status of your pension fund. So if you have doubts about the state of your pension fund, read carefully and keep track of any notices you receive about proposed or pending changes in the rules, and don't be bashful about asking direct questions of your plan administrator.

DECISIONS YOU NEED TO MAKE ABOUT PENSION PLANS

"Every decision you make in your working life is a decision about retirement."
—Olena Berg, former Assistant Secretary,
Pension and Welfare Benefits Administration,
U.S. Department of Labor

WHAT KIND OF RETIREMENT PLAN IS BEST FOR ME? In 1997, about half of the people who received a pension in the United States received it from a defined benefit plan. But the proportion of people with a defined benefit plan has declined rapidly—down from 84 percent of employees of companies with more than one hundred workers in 1980—as 401(k)s and other defined contribution plans have grown in popularity.

If you are making a decision about a new job, be sure to learn all you can about pension benefits. If you are choosing between a job that offers a defined benefit plan and one that offers a defined contribution plan, here are some of the pros and cons you may want to consider before making the choice.

Defined Benefit—Pros

• You will be guaranteed a pension of a certain amount of money if you stay with your employer long enough to be vested.

• You know ahead of time exactly what requirements you must meet to qualify for the pension.

• The amount of your pension is unlikely to be affected by fluctuations in the stock market or other investments.

• If your employer closes down the plan or the company goes bankrupt, the Pension Benefit Guaranty Corporation will probably be able to make sure that you receive at least a portion of your expected benefit.

• The risk on investment of your pension money lies with the employer, who is legally responsible for paying your pension even if the plan's investments do not perform well.

Defined Benefit—Cons

• The amount of your pension will not necessarily increase if your company, or the stock market, experiences an economic boom. You could reap large benefits from an Employee Stock Ownership Plan (ESOP) if the company does well; or lose a lot of money in the market if the stocks you buy with your 401(k) decline.

• You must work for your employer for a certain number of years to qualify for a pension. (See page 42 for minimum vesting requirements.) If you expect to leave the job in a year or two, you probably won't accrue any pension benefit.

Defined Contribution—Pros

• You pay no income taxes on the portion of your salary you contribute and do not have to pay taxes on the earnings on those

Lose a Pension?

If you believe you are entitled to a defined benefit pension from a company that has closed down its pension fund, the PBGC may be able to help you find and collect the money.

If you have access to the Internet, start by searching for your name on a list at the PBGC website (http://search.pbgc.gov/) to see if you are listed as a person for whom the PBGC is holding money due to you from a former employer. If you are not listed, try to locate your former employer, give the company your current address, and make sure you are listed in plan records. If you can't find the company, you can request help by writing to the PBGC Pension Search Program, 1200 K St. N.W., Suite 930, Washington, D.C. 20005-4026, or searching on the website at http://missingpbgc.gov.

When you contact PBGC, include the following information about yourself: your name, address, daytime phone number, Social Security number, date of birth, and, if possible, the dates you worked for the employer. Include as much as possible of the following information about the employer and the plan: the plan's name, nine-digit Employer Identification Number and three-digit plan number, and the name and address of the plan administrator or other representative.

This could be worth your time: In its first four years, the Pension Search program has located about 6,600 people eligible for $21 million in pension benefits. The PBGC says that of the "missing" participants still on their list, more than half are from these six states: California, New York, Texas, New Jersey, Michigan, and Illinois.

contributions until you withdraw the money. When you start withdrawing the money, you pay regular income tax rates, not capital gains taxes.

- You may be allowed to contribute your own money, in addition to your salary, to the plan. This could increase the amount available when you retire.
- Many employers will match a percentage of your contributions.
- You will probably have more control over investment of your savings, since most plans offer you a choice among investment options.
- Your benefits may increase if your investments do well.
- You own and may withdraw all of the money you personally contribute to your 401(k) or similar plan before you retire or leave your current job. (However, you may not be able to avoid tax penalties if you do so.)
- In case of emergency, you may be able to withdraw funds or arrange a loan from your 401(k) at more favorable terms than on the open market.

Defined Contribution—Cons

- Your benefits may decrease if your investments do not do well.
- Unless your employer violates ERISA's rules, you—not your company—are completely responsible for any losses on your investments.
- Employers do not always provide sufficient information for you to make the best investment choices for yourself. This places the burden on you to educate yourself about issues such as asset allocation.
- The money in your plan is not insured by the Pension Benefit Guaranty Corporation.

HOW MUCH MONEY SHOULD I PUT INTO MY 401(K) OR OTHER DEFINED CONTRIBUTION PLAN?

The most effective way to build your savings in a 401(k) or similar plan is to contribute a share of your salary on a regular basis

Pension Alert for Women

Women are less likely than men to have a pension, and when they do have one, the average size of the pension is lower than a man's. Of retirees who are sixty-five or older, 38 percent of women receive some type of pension, compared with 58 percent of men. The average annual pension benefit for women is $5,230; for men, $11,784. In general women's retirement income—including their average Social Security benefits—lags significantly below that of men. This problem is compounded by the fact that women live longer than men, and therefore need more financial resources.

There are many reasons for this pension gap, some of which were discussed in Chapter One. Among them are:

• The earnings gap: women on average earn about seventy-four cents for every dollar earned by men;

• Fewer years in the work force, often as a result of staying at home to meet child care needs; and

• More part-time or sporadic employment than men.

WHAT WOMEN NEED TO DO TO ENSURE THEIR RETIREMENT SECURITY

• Insist on equal pay for equal work. Many pension plans base benefits on salary. The longer you are underpaid, the lower your eventual benefit will be.

• Start saving for your retirement as soon as you start working. If your employer does not offer a pension, save a certain amount of your salary from every pay period in a tax-favored retirement account.

• Save as much as you can in the retirement account, and do not take it out before you retire.

and allow the earnings to compound over many years (see the chart on page 80). To make the most of your 401(k), try to put in at least the maximum tax-deductible contribution every year. If you can't afford to sock away the maximum annual payment, try to contribute at least the amount that your employer is willing to match. Nationally, this averages about 6 percent of your salary.

HOW SHOULD I INVEST THE MONEY IN MY 401(K) OR OTHER DEFINED CONTRIBUTION PLAN?

Here's a true story, told by a pension plan manager, that you do not want to emulate. An employee of a large company opened a 401(k) and checked a box on the enrollment form indicating that she wanted to put all of the money into one mutual fund. For many years she did not pay attention to the annual account statements she received. Suddenly she realized that she had more than $100,000 in that one fund, and no other assets. The employee went to her plan administrator and begged him to suggest ways to diversify her account. Luckily, this employee's choice had provided a decent return. But if she'd chosen unwisely, her retirement savings could have eroded dramatically.

"The most critical decision" you'll have to make, Olena Berg (former Assistant Secretary, Pension and Welfare Benefits Administration, U.S. Department of Labor) advises, "is asset allocation. Ninety percent of the money you make in your defined contribution often depends on the first decision you make." That's because over a period of years, the importance of that decision will be compounded as your earnings—or losses—on stocks, bonds, or other investments compound.

Most 401(k) plans provide several options for investing your money, including stocks, bonds, mutual funds, and government bonds. Before deciding how to apportion your savings among various investments, ask your plan administrator for all available information about your options. If you don't understand the information, seek help from the administrator or, if necessary, from another financial advisor. Employees of large companies often have access to financial education or planning tools—

such as asset allocation models—as well as information about specific investment options.

How you invest your retirement savings, Berg says, should depend on your tolerance for risk. You also need to consider how active you'll be in managing your account. If you keep close tabs on the markets, you may thrive with a retirement account that allows you to participate in the markets on a daily basis. But if you prefer not to monitor so closely, you may want to choose investments that are less likely to be volatile.

SHOULD I TAKE MONEY OUT OF MY PENSION PLAN BEFORE I RETIRE?

If you have a financial crisis or a special need, such as becoming disabled or needing a down payment for a new home or college tuition for one of your children, should you withdraw money from your pension plan to pay for it?

Your 401(k) plan may allow you to take money out for certain hardships while you are still on the job, but the effects can be painful. If you withdraw money before you are fifty-nine and a half, you'll be hit by a double whammy: you'll have to pay income tax on the amount withdrawn, plus an additional penalty of 10 percent. And of course there will also be a hidden penalty—the future, compounded earnings you'll sacrifice to the more immediate priority. (See Chapter Three for information on tax-free early withdrawal of funds from your IRA for specific purposes.)

You may be able to avoid the 10 percent penalty, but not the tax, if you need to withdraw some of your 401(k) funds for certain "hardships," including meeting medical needs. But be sure to ask your plan administrator for information about the IRS's detailed requirements *before* taking the money out.

If your plan permits it, another option is to take a *loan* from your 401(k). The law permits you to borrow up to 50 percent of the money already vested, but no more than $50,000. However, there are some good reasons to try to avoid borrowing from your 401(k) before retirement.

Before You Borrow From a 401(k)

The General Accounting Office (GAO), an agency that studies government programs at the request of Congress, developed the following scenario:

Over the course of a thirty-five-year career, a plan participant contributed 6.8 percent of his or her annual salary, for an annual return of 11 percent on the investment. In the fifteenth year, with $80,000 in the account, the participant took out a loan of $40,000, to be paid back in equal installments over ten years.

Chart 2-A on the next page shows that if the participant did not borrow money, there would be $952,977 in the 401(k) at the time he or she retired. The amount that would be in the account at retirement time if the participant took a loan, however, ranged from $932,968 to as low as $687,863. Two key factors account for the difference in the savings: the interest rate paid by the borrower, and *whether the borrower continued to make regular contributions to the account while paying off the loan.*

- Interest rates on these loans tend to be relatively low and this appears to be attractive. However, this means that the interest you pay back to yourself may be less than the earnings you would receive if you invested that same amount of money elsewhere.
- The law requires you to pay back the loan, including interest, in five years. If you do not pay it all back by the deadline, IRS will tax the amount you still owe as if it were an early withdrawal—at your tax rate plus 10 percent.
- Any money you withdraw for a purpose other than retirement (except for "hardships" mentioned earlier) will reduce the benefit you'd get from compounding earnings on your savings.

Chart 2-A

Impact of Borrowing from a 401(k)		
	Account balance in year 35	Percent of no-loan balance
No loan	$952,977	
Maintain contributions to pension account during loan repayment		
6.3%loan	$892,209	93.6%
7.0% loan	$900,892	94.5%
8.0% loan	$913,526	95.9%
9.5% loan	$932,968	97.9%
Suspend contributions to pension account during loan repayment		
6.3% loan	$687,863	72.2%
7.0% loan	$696,546	73.1%
8.0% loan	$709,180	74.4%
9.5% loan	$728,622	76.5%

Extracted from 401(k) Pension Plans: Loan Provisions Enhance Participation But May Affect Income Security for Some, a report of the General Accounting Office to the Chairman, Special Committee on Aging, and the Honorable Judd Gregg, U.S. Senate, October, 1997.

• The worst case: if you borrow the money and do not make regular contributions to the 401(k) while paying back the loan, your loss of savings could be substantial. Chart 2-A on page 62 shows how this could happen.

WHAT SHOULD I DO WITH MY RETIREMENT SAVINGS IF I CHANGE JOBS?

When you leave your job, if your benefit is worth $5,000 or less, your employer may require you to take it out of the company plan. Some employers, however, will let you leave your 401(k) money in the current account. If you have the choice, compare the investment options in your new plan with those in the company you are leaving, and make a decision based on where you think you'll do better.

However, if you take a lump sum out of a retirement account before you are fifty-nine and a half, you will have to pay taxes on it unless you arrange a "rollover" of the money into an Individual Retirement Account (IRA) or into your new employer's plan. Before you do this, talk to the manager of the company you are leaving, because you must transfer the money directly from one account to the other. If you withdraw a lump sum and put it into your ordinary bank account, and postpone rolling it over to an IRA after sixty days, you will have to pay a 10 percent penalty and your employer will need to withhold 20 percent of the funds for taxes, which you won't be able to get back until you file your tax return for the next year.

You can avoid the 20 percent automatic withholding on the transfer of funds in one of three ways:

• Have the money transferred directly to your new employer's plan;

• Have the money transferred to an IRA you have set up with a bank, a broker, or other organization that sponsors IRAs; or

• Have your employer write a check for the funds in your account that is directly payable to an IRA that you've already set up, not to you personally.

Even if you withdraw the money from your 401(k) or similar account personally, you may still deposit the funds into an IRA and even add back the 20 percent amount that was withheld, so long as you do so within sixty days after you receive it. If you put the full amount back into the IRA you will not owe taxes or the 10 percent penalty. People who are laid off from a job and do not yet have a new one have only one option: transfer the money into an IRA. In any case, make sure your employer follows the strict federal requirements so that you avoid paying unnecessary taxes on the money.

THE TAX FACTOR

The government encourages you to save money for retirement by offering tax breaks for contributions to retirement plans. In return for those tax breaks you must pay hefty penalties if you do not adhere to strict rules about how and when you can withdraw your retirement savings.

While you are still working, you do not have to pay taxes on the money you or your employer puts into your pension fund. However, you must pay income taxes on your pension when you start receiving it. Here's a brief description of the tax treatment of the money you put into your retirement plan, and the money you take out:

Money In
The contributions to a defined benefit plan come from your employer, and you do not have to pay a tax on these at the time they go into the pension fund.

If you participate in a defined contribution plan such as a 401(k), you may defer income tax on the money when you contribute it to the account, up to a limit the government sets each year. In 2001, the limit is $10,500 for a 401(k).

Some retirement plans allow you to put more than the limit into your account annually, but you will not be able to deduct those contributions on your income tax.

Money Out

Until you turn fifty-nine and a half, taking money out of your pension fund is expensive. It can also be expensive if you wait until after you turn seventy and a half.

In general, if you withdraw money before you're fifty-nine and a half, Uncle Sam will charge you a penalty of 10 percent on the amount withdrawn, in addition to regular income tax, unless you incur a disability or other hardship. (For details on exceptions, see IRS Publication 575, "Pension and Annuity Income.") Once you are older, however, you will pay only regular income tax—not the capital gains rate—on the pension you receive in the form of, for example, a monthly check, or the lump-sum you withdraw from your 401(k). Because most people's incomes decline when they retire, you are likely to benefit from paying at a lower tax rate than if you were still working.

If you change jobs and are required or want to take your pension money out of your former employer's fund, you may avoid the penalty by doing what is called a "rollover"—putting the money into your new employer's plan (if that is allowed), or into an Individual Retirement Account.

If you have other retirement income and do not want to withdraw money from your defined contribution plan or IRA sooner, you can postpone what the government calls a "distribution" until you reach age seventy and a half. Once you reach that age, Uncle Sam requires you to start withdrawing the money according to a formula based on your age. If you don't do this, you'll have to pay a 50 percent penalty on the amount you were supposed to withdraw. An important exception: if you continue to work past seventy and a half, you don't have to take a distribution from the plan of your current employer as long as you are working, which means you can continue to benefit from the tax-deferred earnings on your nest egg.

* * *

If you feel exhausted or confused by trying to wade through the details of Uncle Sam's role in overseeing your pension, it's only natural. No one can master, let alone remember, all of the details. Now that you have an overview of how the system works, there are really only four main points to remember.

• The pension plans offered by most employers must abide by certain federal requirements.

• Before deciding which plan to choose and/or how to invest the money in your plan, make sure you have all the information you need to figure out the options that will work best for you and your family.

• If you suspect that your plan is not being properly managed, or if you cannot get information about it, you have rights to both information and legal action under federal law.

• It's best *not* to take money out of your pension plan before you retire, if you can help it.

FOR MORE INFORMATION

BY TELEPHONE

AARP
Order their free booklets, "Your Pension Plan: A Guide to Getting Through the Maze" (AARP Stock D13533) and "Your 401(k) Plan: Building Toward Your Retirement Security" (D15975), by calling 1-800-424-3410.

Pension Benefit Guaranty Corporation (PBGC)
The PBGC guarantees payment of pension benefits of workers covered by defined benefit plans that terminate. Call the Customer Service Center at 1-800-400-PBGC for information on eligibility and applying for benefits.

U.S. Department of Labor (USDOL)
For a list of very useful free publications call 1-800-998-7542. Titles you can order include "Protect Your Pension," "What You Should Know About Your Pension Rights," and "Women and Pensions: What Women Need to Know and Do."

BY MAIL

Pension and Welfare Benefits Administration (PWBA)

The Form 5500 that employers must file with PWBA contains detailed financial information on the company's pension plan. You can order a copy of your plan, or any other company's, by writing to the U.S. Department of Labor, PWBA Office of Public Disclosure, Room N-1513, 200 Constitution Ave. N.W., Washington, DC 20210. You will be charged fifteen cents per photocopied page.

ON THE INTERNET

www.pbgc.gov

If you have a defined benefit pension, contact this site for information on what the Pension Benefit Guaranty Corporation is doing to protect it. Click on "Publications" for a list of helpful brochures and documents from both PBGC and the Labor Department.

http://search.pbgc.gov

PBGC operates a clearinghouse for locating missing participants and beneficiaries in PBGC-insured defined benefit pension plans that close down. From this site you can order a fact sheet on PBGC's "Missing Participants Program." If your name is listed in the Pension Search Directory located on the website, or you are a survivor of a person on the list, you should call 1-800-326-LOST to request an application for pension benefits that you may be owed.

www.dol.gov/dol/pwba

This site offers information on programs and publications of the PWBA, which administers ERISA. Publications found here are the same titles you can order by calling the USDOL's toll-free phone number, mentioned earlier.

CHAPTER THREE

Saving for Retirement

"I am sixty-seven years old and retired," said the man we'll call Jim, when he made a telephone call to the U.S. Department of Labor. "I am getting up in the morning and flipping hamburgers at a fast-food restaurant. I worked my whole life—I feel like I've been cheated."

Jim was working during his "retirement" because it was the only way to make ends meet. When the Department looked into his background, they found that on his first job, there was no pension benefit. On his second job, Jim stayed long enough to vest his benefits, but they were very meager. He left his third job before the pension benefits were vested, and went to work for an employer who offered a 401(k) savings plan. But by then Jim's kids were in school, resources were tight, and although he received information about the 401(k), he did not put any money into it.

Stories such as Jim's are all too common. People who have worked diligently their entire lives have either neglected to think about retirement or to make choices that would offer them more financial security in the future.

However, there is some good news: As more questions have been raised about the long-term solvency of Social Security, the government has been creating more incentives to encourage you to save for retirement. These are in the form of tax breaks through the IRA, SEP, Keogh plans, and other special plans. The incentives are not subsidies or outright grants, explains Olena Berg, former Assistant Secretary for the Pension and Welfare Benefits Administration of the Labor Department, but they are important tools to help you maintain a regular savings program. The philosophy behind current federal retirement policy, she explains, is to give people the tools required, but make them responsible for using them to set up their own savings program.

What are these plans, which one is best for you, and how can you maximize your benefits from them? (Because all of the options discussed in this chapter are essentially tax breaks, there is no separate section on "The Tax Factor," as in most other chapters of this book.)

WHAT YOU NEED TO KNOW ABOUT RETIREMENT SAVINGS

As a result of laws passed in 1996 and 1997, the spectrum of tax-favored retirement savings options has increased significantly. The only downside to this is that there are now so many different vehicles, it's not always easy to figure out which ones you qualify for, let alone which one(s) are likely to benefit you the most.

Your options for saving for retirement vary, depending on whether you already have access to a pension, 401(k), or other savings program through your employer; whether you are self-employed or the owner of a small business; and on your income and family status. Each alternative also has its own rules about how much money you are allowed to contribute each year, and how much of that contribution may be tax-deductible.

This section gives you a nuts-and-bolts, basic description of the savings choices that offer tax incentives. (It does not cover other, regular savings in a regular bank or brokerage account for which you do not receive a tax break.) The information is intended to serve as an overview, to give you an idea of the types of retirement accounts that are available. The section "Decisions You Need to Make," on page 78, offers tips on how to figure out, among the accounts you qualify for, which type is best for you.

THE BASICS OF INDIVIDUAL RETIREMENT ACCOUNTS (IRAS)

IRAs are probably the most familiar retirement savings account, and the easiest to set up, so many people have been contributing to IRAs throughout their work life. IRAs offer great flexibility for investment. It is easy to put off saving for months and then, at the end of the year, to simply stash some money in an IRA at your local bank or in a CD or mutual fund that advertises an attractive return in the newspapers. As a result, some people end up with many IRA accounts, located in various financial institutions.

Stan Hinden, a business reporter for *The Washington Post,* learned about the pitfalls of this approach firsthand when he retired: "Over the years," Hinden wrote in the *Post,* "I accumulated a number of IRAs—but did so in a willy-nilly fashion, putting them in different fund companies and banks. I realized too late that it's not only how much you save, but also how you organize your investments that can make a real difference in what you take into retirement."

There are two main strategies for avoiding what happened to Hinden. One is to resolve that, if you do want to choose the most attractive IRA each year, you will analyze your holdings at least annually to determine whether you need to shift or combine some of the investments. The other option is to open one IRA account, say with a brokerage house or a bank that offers a range of investment choices—stocks, bonds, mutual funds, CDs, etc.—within that account. Then you'll get one statement with all of your IRA holdings, and you'll be able to trade or shift investments more easily.

Hinden's words of wisdom have more validity today than they would have only a couple of years ago, because there are now more types of IRAs, and more alternatives to IRAs, than in the past. Figuring out how to manage your savings to your greatest advantage poses more of a challenge than ever. The first step is to understand the general rules of IRAs—how they are the same and then, the variations on the major IRA themes.

All IRAs have the following in common:

• You may open an IRA if you received taxable earnings from your work during the year and are no older than seventy and a half at the end of the year. (The exception to this is the spousal IRA; see page 75.)

• You contribute money to an account that is in your name and is managed by you.

• The maximum IRA contribution you can deduct from your income tax is currently the lesser of the amount of income you earn for the year or $2,000. You may make contributions to an IRA for a given tax year until April 15 of the next year, and receive a deduction on the previous year's taxes. For example, if you put money into your IRA on April 14, 2001 you may receive a deduction on the 1998 taxes you pay on April 15, 2001.

• Even if you have several different IRAs, you may only contribute a total of $2,000 per year.

• You or your employer may set up your IRA account in a bank, a brokerage firm, a credit union, or other financial institution. Investment options for an IRA include everything from an interest-bearing bank account to CDs, stocks, bonds, and mutual funds.

• With few exceptions, if you take money out of your account before you are fifty-nine and a half years old, you must pay a 10 percent penalty for early withdrawal. In addition, you may have 20 percent of the IRA funds withheld for income tax until you have paid your tax for the current year.

• You must begin to take money out of your IRA account no later than April 1 of the year after you turn seventy and a half.

• As Stan Hinden learned, the amount of money that accumulates in your IRA depends on your own investment choices and how you manage them. Unless you have a broker who follows and manages your accounts actively, the responsibility for maximizing your earnings is all your own.

Now let's look at what various types of IRAs do *not* have in common: their rules of eligibility and the nature of the tax breaks they offer.

Deductible IRA

In addition to participating in your employer's pension plan, you may also put money into an IRA. However, the amount you may contribute phases out according to a formula based on your income. In 2001 you may contribute to a deductible IRA if your income is $43,000 or less for an individual and $63,000 or less for a married couple filing jointly. The limit will increase annually until 2007, when the limit for singles will be $60,000 and $100,000 for married couples.

Non-deductible IRA Contributions

If you do not qualify to make a deductible IRA contribution (or a Roth IRA contribution, as described below), you may make a non-deductible contribution as long as your total contribution is no more than $2,000. This strategy allows the IRA earnings to grow on a tax-deferred basis, but you will have to pay tax on those earnings when you withdraw the money. Since you will already have paid taxes on part of your IRA holdings, you will need to keep track of this on a special tax form (Form 8606) that you file with your annual return. This way you can avoid being taxed a second time on contributions for which you have already paid the taxes.

Payroll Deduction IRA

This type of IRA is most common in a small business, when the company owner collects a portion of the employee's salary from each pay period and deposits it directly into an IRA account. How much you contribute is up to you, and you can still get a deduction for up to $2,000 per year. The employer decides where to locate the account, and sets it up in your name.

Roth or "Backloaded" IRA

This IRA takes its name from former U.S. Senator William Roth (R.-Del.), who proposed the idea in Congress. It's referred to as "backloaded" because you cannot claim an income tax deduction when you put money into it. However, when you withdraw the money—plus the earnings on your investments—you pay no income tax on it if the account is at least five years old and you are either fifty-nine and a half years old or you use the money you withdrew for certain purposes that the IRS allows. (See the section on withdrawals, page 76.)

Unlike the deductible version, the Roth IRA does not require you to stop contributing at age seventy and a half, or start withdrawing money at that time. This makes it a good vehicle for savings that you intend to pass on to children or other heirs.

The total amount you may put into a Roth IRA each year is $2,000, minus the amount you contribute to other deductible IRAs in the same year. Individuals may put money into a Roth IRA if their income is $110,000 or less, and married couples if it's $160,000 or less.

SEP-IRA

See Simplified Employee Pension plan on page 76. The SEP is sometimes also referred to as a SEP-IRA.

SIMPLE IRA

If you work for or own a small business, you know it's hard to get or to provide the retirement and other benefits that are commonplace if you work for large employers. That's why the government recently created the concept of "SIMPLE" plans—available to employers of one hundred or fewer employees—that encourage retirement savings, yet require less paperwork than the other options already on the books. (The acronym stands for Savings Incentive Match Plan for Employees of Small Employers.)

One type of SIMPLE plan is a new IRA created by the 1996 tax law. The advantage of a SIMPLE IRA is that you may contribute up to $6,500 in 2001. Your employer is required to contribute to your account, but may choose between two options: contributing up to 3 percent of your salary, or contributing 2 percent of the pay of all of the company's eligible employees.

A SIMPLE plan must offer you a sixty-day enrollment period, usually at the beginning of the year. You may decide whether to put your IRA savings into an account chosen by the employer, or into a different financial institution of your choice. As with other IRAs, if you take money out before you turn fifty-nine and a half, you'll pay a 10 percent penalty. In addition, if you try to withdraw money less than two years after you open the account you'll have to pay a 25 percent tax on it.

Spousal IRA

Sandy and Roger have been saving every month for their retirement, but they also feel strongly that Sandy should stay home to care for their new baby for at least a couple of years. Roger's enrolled in a pension plan at work. But Sandy will have to quit her job, and this means that she won't be able to make tax-deductible contributions to her 401(k) as long as she is not working.

Until the 1997 tax law passed, if Sandy did not earn any income, she could not contribute to an IRA because Roger already participated in a pension plan. Now the law has changed. A non-working spouse—or a spouse who is employed but not covered by an employer pension plan—has the right to set up and contribute up to $2,000 per year to a deductible IRA, as long as the couple's income is no more than $160,000.

Keogh Plans

You can use a Keogh plan for tax-deductible retirement savings if you are self-employed or if you are a sole proprietor or partner in a business. A Keogh can take the form of either a defined benefit or defined contribution plan (see Chapter Two), and the form determines the amount of deductible contributions allowed in a given year. There are different types of Keoghs, with different contribution limits and deadlines. To figure out if a Keogh is for you, and how large a contribution you may make in a given year, you'll need an accountant or other expert to crunch the numbers of some complicated formulas. A key factor to consider is that if you have employees, you must set up a plan for them as well as for yourself. If you have a Keogh plan, as in the case of an IRA, you'll need to start taking money out of it by April 1 of the year after you turn seventy and a half. At that time, you'll have to pay income tax on the withdrawal.

Simplified Employee Pension (SEP) Plan

Like a Keogh, a SEP may be used by a person who is self-employed, or may be established by a small business for its employees. If you work for yourself and do not require the potential for higher tax-deductible contributions offered by a Keogh, you'll find the SEP a less complicated way to save for retirement. If you're self-employed, you may contribute 13.045 percent of your income or $30,000, whichever is lower. If you own a small business, you can create a SEP for your employees and make a tax-deductible contribution of up to 15 percent of their salaries or $24,000 to the account for each employee. To qualify, your business must have no more than one hundred employees who earned $5,000 or more in the previous year.

SIMPLE 401(k)

Like the SIMPLE IRA, this type of plan, designed for small businesses, was created in 1996 as a more streamlined vehicle for retirement savings by owners and employees of small businesses. If your employer offers a SIMPLE 401(k), you may be able to save up to $10,500 per year in this account, depending on your salary.

WITHDRAWING YOUR RETIREMENT SAVINGS

Most tax-favored retirement savings plans impose a penalty if you withdraw money before you are fifty-nine and a half, and if you do not start withdrawing the money by April 1 of the year you turn seventy and a half. The IRS calls the money you take out of these plans "distributions." Before you retire, you may remove money, say, from a 401(k) and put it into an IRA, or shift it from one IRA to another, without penalty, if you follow certain strict IRS rules. This is called a "rollover."

The rules and formulas for rollovers and distributions are very complicated and, of course, there are some exceptions. Here is a summary of the most important, most basic facts to help you decide which savings vehicles to use and when to start taking money out.

IRAs in General

If you withdraw money before you turn fifty-nine and a half, you must pay a penalty of 10 percent in addition to the regular income tax on the amount withdrawn. By April 1 of the year after you turn seventy and a half, you must withdraw the money in your IRA in one of two ways: take all of it out, or begin to receive a certain minimum distribution based on a formula that takes into account your age and projected lifespan. When you receive the money, you pay ordinary income tax on it.

Your Existing IRA

You do not have to pay a penalty for early withdrawals if they are for medical expenses which consist of more than 7.5 percent of your income, or for the following additional purposes: if you become disabled and cannot work; to pay higher education expenses of yourself, your spouse, children, or grandchildren; if you have been receiving unemployment benefits for more than twelve weeks; or, up to a $10,000 limit, to help buy a first-time home for yourself or a close relative.

Roth IRA

Once you have had a Roth IRA for five years, you may withdraw funds before age fifty-nine and a half without penalty for the same purposes listed in the section above, "Your Existing IRA." Unlike other retirement accounts, you do not have to start taking money out of this IRA when you are seventy and a half.

SIMPLE IRA

If you withdraw money before you have had the account for two years, you must pay a 25 percent penalty. Other distribution rules are the same as for IRAs in general.

Keogh Plan
Exceptions to the 10 percent penalty for early withdrawals
include: payment to your beneficiary if you die; disability; payment for medical care up to the amount of the medical expense
deduction; or, in certain cases, if you leave your employer to
retire or take another job.

SEPs
The rules are the same as for the regular IRA, as described
above.

DECISIONS YOU NEED TO MAKE

Who should contribute to a tax-favored retirement savings
plan? Pretty much every American worker who hopes to have a
comfortable retirement. There are three types of workers who
stand to benefit from these plans: employees of companies that
offer a pension or retirement savings plan such as a 401(k), self-
employed people, and small business owners.

If You're an Employee
Even if you know that your employer will pay you a pension
when you retire, or you are contributing regularly to a 401(k)
or similar plan at work, you may still want to take advantage of
your working years to save more money in some other type of
tax-favored plan. Here are just a few reasons:
  • Your pension alone, even when added to Social Security,
may produce less retirement income than you want or need;
  • There is an annual limit on the amount of tax-deductible
contributions you can make to a 401(k) or other defined contribution plan; and
  • You may be dissatisfied with the investment options or
returns in your 401(k) or other employer plan, and would prefer to invest additional money elsewhere. (If this is your reason—unless the return is extremely low—you should still prob-

ably contribute as much money as your employer will match each year.)

If You're Self-employed
If you have been self-employed for any time at all—or are considering becoming self-employed—you should give serious attention to how to save for your retirement. Social Security rarely provides enough income to be comfortable, and you lack the luxury of an employer who is contributing to your nest egg. The size of your retirement income is entirely up to you, and the sooner you start saving, the greater your nest egg will be.

If You're a Small Business Owner
According to the Labor Department, in 1996 about 46 percent of full-time employees of small businesses had pension coverage, compared to 80 percent of workers in businesses with one hundred or more employees in 1997. If you're one of those workers who is not covered, you should encourage your employer to consider setting up one of the new "SIMPLE" pension plans, which can be in the form of an IRA or a 401(k), so that you can benefit from your employer's contribution as well as your own.

If You're a Woman
Women, of course, may belong to any of the above categories. But they lag significantly behind men in retirement income. Reasons for this include that they receive lower wages than men—72 cents to the dollar in 1999, according to the Labor Department—and that they are more likely than men to work part-time or take time out of the labor force for child and elder care. As a result, women on average receive lower Social Security and pension benefits than men, and are less likely to have a pension. These facts reinforce the importance for women of beginning as early as possible to save as much as they can afford for retirement.

Here are some of the key questions and factors to consider in making decisions about saving for your retirement.

Starting Early

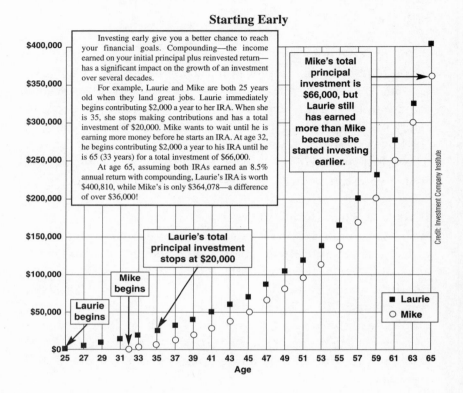

Investing early give you a better chance to reach your financial goals. Compounding—the income earned on your initial principal plus reinvested return—has a significant impact on the growth of an investment over several decades.

For example, Laurie and Mike are both 25 years old when they land great jobs. Laurie immediately begins contributing $2,000 a year to her IRA. When she is 35, she stops making contributions and has a total investment of $20,000. Mike wants to wait until he is earning more money before he starts an IRA. At age 32, he begins contributing $2,000 a year to his IRA until he is 65 (33 years) for a total investment of $66,000.

At age 65, assuming both IRAs earned an 8.5% annual return with compounding, Laurie's IRA is worth $400,810, while Mike's is only $364,078—a difference of over $36,000!

Mike's total principal investment is $66,000, but Laurie still has earned more than Mike because she started investing earlier.

Laurie's total principal investment stops at $20,000

Mike begins

Laurie begins

■ Laurie
○ Mike

Credit: Investment Company Institute

Age

SHOULD I PARTICIPATE IN A RETIREMENT SAVINGS PLAN?

Don't let this happen to you: A sixty-seven-year-old worker recently called the Labor Department for information. "I have just retired," he said. "Where is the government agency I call to get my pension?"

The answer, of course, is that there is no government agency—unless you count Social Security—that will pay you a pension. Hopefully by now most Americans are informed about whether they will receive a pension from their employer. But that's not the end of the story. How much money you have to live on in retirement depends increasingly on how far-sighted and diligent you are about setting up a savings plan and sticking to it. Because the earnings are compounded over a longer period of time, "one dollar you put to work for your retirement in your early twenties or thirties is much more effective" than money you save later in life, advises Olena Berg, formerly of the Labor Department.

But even if you are older than thirty—or older than fifty— the principle remains the same: *The sooner you save and the more you save, the more resources you'll have to live on when you retire.*

HOW MUCH SHOULD I CONTRIBUTE TO MY RETIREMENT SAVINGS?

Most financial advisors agree on the answer: "As much as you can afford," taking as much advantage as possible of the tax deductions and deferrals that Uncle Sam offers. If you want to stash away more than the law allows in the types of accounts

---

How Much Do I Need to Save for Retirement?

You can protect yourself against future shortfalls by calculating how much you need to save for retirement as many years ahead as possible.

The American Savings Education Council, a coalition of companies, non-profit organizations, and government agencies that encourages saving for retirement, publishes a "Ballpark Estimate" worksheet that you can use to calculate the amount you'll need to put away annually to achieve your goal. You can order a copy of the worksheet by sending a business envelope with ninety-nine cents postage to ASEC at 2121 K St. N.W., Suite 600, Washington, DC, or do the calculations on the Internet through ASEC's website, http://www.asec.org/.

You can also ask your broker, financial planner, or other adviser for a form that will help you itemize costs of housing, transportation, and other basic expenses to help you arrive at the amount of income you'll need.

described in this chapter, you need to talk to a financial advisor about the other types of investments available to you, and their tax consequences.

I HAVE A JOB THAT WILL PROVIDE ME WITH A PENSION WHEN I RETIRE. WHAT TAX-FAVORED SAVINGS OPTIONS DO I HAVE?

The choices you and your spouse have are all IRAs—the deductible version, the Roth IRA, and the spousal IRA. In any case, the maximum tax-free contribution you'll be able to make each year is $2,000. For a married couple with one non-working spouse, the total could be $4,000—$2,000 each in a spousal IRA and one other type of IRA. The most difficult decision you'll face is whether to choose a deductible IRA or a Roth IRA, and there's no easy answer. If you need more tax deductions immediately, the deductible IRA may be the answer for you. However, you should know that the type of IRA that's better for you in the long run depends on several factors: your current tax bracket, the bracket you'll be in when you retire, how much money you save, and the amount of return on those investments. In many cases, putting your money into a Roth IRA will produce a greater return over time. To answer the question, you'll need to ask your accountant, broker, or other financial advisor to crunch the numbers for you.

If you are going to put savings into IRAs, Scott M. Kahan, a certified financial planner and president of Financial Asset Management Corp. in New York, cautions you to consolidate them into one or at least very few accounts, to avoid dealing with the complicated formulas the IRS applies to taxing these savings when you start withdrawing the money. "People don't realize the nightmare they are creating when they start pulling money out (for retirement) if they have a lot of different IRAs," he says, especially if they're putting deductible and non-deductible contributions into the same account. Every year you make non-deductible contributions, you'll have to file Form 8606, "Nondeductible IRS (Contributions, Distributions and Basis)," along with your 1040 and other IRS tax forms.

Finally, if you have income from work outside your primary job—let's say, from consulting—you may take advantage of two other tax-favored options by setting up a SEP or a Keogh.

NEXT YEAR I'M GOING TO LEAVE MY JOB AND WORK FOR MYSELF AS AN INDEPENDENT CONSULTANT. WHAT OPTIONS DO I HAVE FOR RETIREMENT SAVINGS?

If you will not have employees—except for possibly hiring some contract labor to do occasional jobs such as research or data input—your best choice is a Simplified Employee Pension (SEP). A SEP resembles an IRA in its flexibility. You can set one up at a bank, brokerage house, or other financial institution, and you can invest it in a wide range of financial instruments. But your IRA contributions are limited to $2,000 per year, and your SEP contribution may be much more—the lesser of 13.045 percent of your net earnings, or $30,000. Although you are eligible to set up a Keogh plan, the only reason for taking on the extra paperwork would be if you want to get a tax deduction for contributing a higher percentage of your earnings than is allowed by the SEP.

MY WIFE AND I HAVE ALWAYS GIVEN PRIORITY TO PAYING OFF OUR HOME MORTGAGE, FIGURING WE WILL START SAVING FOR RETIREMENT AFTER THAT. IS THIS A GOOD DECISION?

George, forty-five, and Sally, forty-three, moved into a house three years ago and are paying off the mortgage. Since moving into the house, their incomes have increased substantially. George has gone into business for himself, and is considering opening a SEP. Now they're debating: Should they put an extra $250 per month into the SEP, or use it to speed up the payoff of their mortgage?

The primary reason to pay off a mortgage is if you intend to live in the house after you've retired, or to buy another one outright, so that you don't have to worry about a monthly payment. George and Sally, however, do not plan to stay in the house when they retire. Because they bought their house quite recently, they can deduct almost their entire monthly payment as a mortgage interest deduction. George and Sally and many other people will find that they can reap triple benefits from putting the $250 per month into the SEP: reducing their taxes by using the mortgage interest deduction, deducting the annual SEP contribution, and postponing tax on the earnings in the SEP until they withdraw the money for retirement.

*   *   *

Uncle Sam offers a smorgasbord of savings accounts that provide you immediate benefits in the form of a tax deduction or deferral, and long-term benefits—if you have invested wisely—in the form of more assets to draw on for your retirement. Unfortunately, as these accounts have proliferated, the numbers you must calculate to determine your eligibility, contributions, and withdrawals have become as complicated as their names. If you qualify for more than one type of account, you should ask the person in charge of your plan at work, or some other type of financial advisor, to help you choose the one that is most beneficial for you.

In the meantime, keep the following key facts about tax-favored retirement accounts in mind.

• The earlier you start to save, the more assets you'll have for retirement.

• Although it is the most familiar form of retirement account, the regular deductible IRA may not be the best for you. That's because your annual tax-deductible contribution is limited to $2,000 per year. So you need to consider all the options for which you are eligible.

• Eligibility requirements and contribution limits change for some of these accounts every year. Be sure to monitor your accounts and conduct a thorough evaluation at least annually to make sure your current choices are giving you the biggest bang for the buck.

FOR MORE INFORMATION

BY TELEPHONE

Internal Revenue Service (IRS)
"Circular E, Employer's Tax Guide" (Publication 15), describes the tax laws that affect SIMPLE plans. Other key IRS publications, all free, that deal with retirement savings include the "Older Americans' Tax Guide" (Pub. 554), "Retirement Plans for Small Business" (Pub. 560), "Pension and Annuity Income" (Pub. 575), and "Individual Retirement Arrangements (IRAs)" (Pub. 590). You can order them by calling the IRS toll-free at 1-800-829-3676 (TTY/TDD 1-800-829-4059). From your FAX machine, dial 703-368-9694.

U.S. Department of Labor (USDOL) Pension and Welfare Benefits Administration (PWBA)
To learn the basics about SIMPLE retirement plans for small business, call PWBA toll-free at 1-800-998-7542 (TDD 1-800-326-2577) and request these brochures: "Simple Retirement Solutions for Small Business," "Simplified Employee Pensions (SEPs): What Small Businesses Need To Know," and "Savings Incentive Match Plans for Employees of Small Employers (SIMPLE)." You may also request a free list of other PWBA publications.

BY MAIL

American Savings Education Council (ASEC)
The purpose of this coalition of corporations, government agencies, and nonprofit organizations is to inform the public about retirement savings and planning. ASEC will send you a packet of free information including a "Ballpark Estimate" worksheet to calculate how much you need to save for retirement, and "How Do I Get There from Here?" a guide to working with brokers, financial planners, and other advisors on retirement

planning and investing. The guide also lists other information sources including publications, television programs, software, and websites. To receive the information packet, send a no. 10 business-size envelope with ninety-nine cents postage to: ASEC Brochures, Suite 600, American Savings Education Council, 2121 K St. N.W., Washington, DC 20037-1896.

USDOL PWBA
Request publications from or send your questions about SIM-PLE plans and other retirement savings programs to: Pension and Welfare Benefits Administration, U.S. Department of Labor, Customer Service Representative, Rm. N-5625, 200 Constitution Ave. N.W., Washington, DC 20210.

ON THE INTERNET

www.asec.org
At ASEC's home page, click on "Savings Tools," then select the interactive version of "Ballpark Estimate" or print out a copy of the worksheet. At this address you can also read "How Do I Get There From Here?," a pamphlet described in the section above. By selecting "Savings Tools," you can get a list of definitions of saving and retirement terms.

www.dol.gov/dol/pwba
Click on "Publications" at PWBA's home page to read the text of the three booklets mentioned above, plus eleven other titles.

www.irs.ustreas.gov
At the home page of the IRS, choose "Forms & Pubs." Then select "Publications" or "Forms and Instructions." To retrieve any of the five publications under the "by phone" section, select a file format and the file you wish to read. Then decide whether you want to read the file online or download it, and press the appropriate button.

CHAPTER FOUR

Protecting and Preserving Your Job (for as long as you want it)

At fifty-nine, Bill was a healthy, active department head at Ajax, Inc., where he had worked for thirty-seven years. He was shocked when his boss told him that the company wanted him to take early retirement. He also learned that Ajax was hiring a person who was thirty-five years old for a job that sounded suspiciously similar to his own, at a much lower salary. Bill looked into the law against age discrimination and told his boss that he knew that it was illegal to force someone into retirement solely on the basis of age.

Bill didn't want to continue to work at Ajax after this experience. But by suggesting that he would sue the company for age discrimination, he secured a retirement package that was much better than the original offer.

Are you being pushed toward early retirement against your will? Has your supervisor denied you a salary increase or a promotion, saying that "you are already doing very well for someone your age?"

Federal law says your employer cannot force you to retire early, against your will, just because of your age. It is also illegal for your employer to make decisions about other terms of your employment—such as your salary or your pension benefits—on the basis of your age. This chapter will describe how the law can help you keep your job, your standing in the company, and the salary and benefits you have been counting on until you are ready to retire.

WHAT YOU NEED TO KNOW ABOUT PROTECTING YOUR JOB

The Age Discrimination in Employment Act (ADEA) of 1967, as well as several other government policies enacted more recently, protect you against age discrimination on the job if you are forty or older, and work for a company with at least twenty employees or for federal or local government. (Some state laws go further, prohibiting job discrimination in businesses with only fifteen employees.) In a March 2000 decision, the U.S. Supreme Court ruled that state employees were not protected by the ADEA, so if you fall into this category, you must pursue your claim of age discrimination through the appropriate state office. (You can get information on how to do this by contacting the Equal Employment Opportunity Commission, as described on page 92.)

The federal law specifically forbids employers to practice age discrimination in the following areas:

• Hiring;
• Firing;
• Compensation;
• Benefits, such as your pension plan; and
• Any other "terms or conditions" of your employment.

It is also illegal for employers to:

• List age as a qualification in an advertisement for a job opening; and

• Retaliate against a worker who files an age discrimination charge or who assists in investigation or testifies in a legal proceeding on such a charge.

The law also prohibits age discrimination in employment by employment agencies and labor unions.

Two aspects of the law are especially important to know about as you approach retirement: how the law protects your pension and other benefits, and what rights you have if you are offered an early retirement incentive plan or buyout.

PROTECTING YOUR PENSION AND OTHER BENEFITS
In general, an employer may not refuse you the right to participate
in a pension or other benefit plan because of your age, unless there
is an actuarial basis for doing so.

One example of a case in which the employer did *not* have
the actuarial verification led to a finding of illegal discrimination. The company, located in Florida, did not allow new
employees to participate in its pension plan if they were forty-
five years or older. Following a lawsuit, they had to open up the
plan to all employees regardless of their age.

Another situation in which age discrimination frequently
crops up is in the benefits that employers include in early retirement or "buyout" offers, often proposed to an individual or
group of employees when a company downsizes. Here's an
example of what can happen: Ajax, Inc., wants to address a cash
flow crisis by offering a buyout. The company says that employees who are willing to retire in July will be treated as if they had
worked for Ajax for the thirty years required to receive a full
pension. Joe has been there twenty-five years, so he would get
five "free" years toward his pension by retiring now. But Sam
has worked for Ajax for twenty-nine years, and would only get
one extra year of credit. This buyout proposal would violate the
ADEA because it would base distribution of benefits on the
employee's age.

EXAMINING EARLY RETIREMENT OFFERS
There are two key facts you need to understand if your company offers you an early retirement package:
  • As a condition for your acceptance of an early retirement
incentive, your employer may ask you to waive your right to
pursue existing claims under the ADEA or other civil rights or
employment laws—but not any future claims.
  • The government requires employers to meet a series of
specific conditions in any waiver the employer asks you to
sign.

Waiving Your Claims

To cut through the legalese, let's consider this example: Ann is fifty years old. She was deputy director of the operations department at Ajax. When her boss left, Ann applied for the job, but she lost it to Barbara, a management trainee who is thirty-eight. Ann filed a complaint of age discrimination against her employer with the EEOC.

Six months later, while the charge was still pending, Ajax offered Ann an early retirement package. Ann decided to take the package and look for another job, because she found it uncomfortable at Ajax, where she was constantly coming into contact with the company officials she was suing. In order to get the benefits she had to sign a waiver of her rights to claims against Ajax, knowing that this meant she could not pursue her pending ADEA case.

After several months of hunting unsuccessfully for a new job, Ann realized that Ajax management was giving her bad references, and telling the companies she applied to that she'd filed suit against them. As a result, Ann filed another charge against Ajax—this one alleging that the company was retaliating against her for filing the previous charge. Because the issue arose after Ann had signed the waiver, she had the legal right to file and pursue the second charge.

Requirements for a Legal Waiver

The law requires that when you decide to sign a waiver of claims against your employer in return for early retirement benefits, your decision be "knowing and voluntary." At a minimum, the waiver must:

- Be in the form of an agreement between you and your employer;
- Be written in a way that you or the average person who is eligible for the early retirement package can understand; and
- Advise you of your right to consult an attorney before you sign.

Waiving Your Right to Sue Your Employer

Dolores M. Oubre worked as a scheduler for a power plant operated by Entergy Operations, Inc., in Killona, Louisiana. When her employer asked her to leave her job, Oubre signed a termination agreement waiving her legal claim against the company and collected $6,258 in severance pay. After collecting the money, she sued the company for age discrimination.

Entergy took Oubre to court, arguing that the employee had given up her claims under the Age Discrimination in Employment Act and had no right to sue. Entergy also requested that the court make Oubre return the money. In a January 1998 decision, the U.S. Supreme Court ruled in Oubre's favor, strongly confirming that an employer cannot enforce a waiver of rights signed by the employee if the company has not met the ADEA legal requirements for the waiver. (See the discussion on page 90.)

In this case, the Court ruled, Entergy had given Oubre only fourteen days, instead of the required twenty-one days, to consider their offer, and it had not given her the required seven days after signing to reject it.

In return for the waiver of your rights, your employer must offer some additional benefit beyond what you are already entitled to. Examples might be a one-time, $1,000 retirement bonus or an extension of your health insurance for a year beyond the legal requirement.

The law also protects you against being forced to make a hasty decision you may regret later. If the early retirement package is being offered only to you, as an individual, you must be given at least twenty-one days to consider it before making a decision. If the package is being offered to a group of employees, each person affected must have at least forty-five days to consider it. In either case, once you've actually signed the agreement, you still have seven days—during which the agreement is not in effect—to revoke it.

When an employer offers a waiver in return for early retirement to a group of employees, as may occur when a particular division is closed or a business merges, the company must offer in writing a description of which employees are eligible for the early retirement package and which are not, including the job titles and ages of workers in each category. The employer must also specify the amount of time eligible employees may have to decide whether to accept the offer.

Unfortunately, individuals who are offered early retirement buyouts do *not* have the right to information about others who may have been offered packages in the past, or the provisions of those offers.

An Exception to the Rules

If you are an executive or hold a "high policy-making position" in your company, you may be an exception to the rule against compulsory retirement. The law permits your employer to require you to retire involuntarily if you are sixty-five years old, if you've worked in a top position for the last two years, and if you're entitled to immediately receive an annual pension of at least $44,000.

HOW TO FIGHT AGE DISCRIMINATION

Filing a Charge

More than forty states have their own age discrimination laws, and some of these are stronger than the federal law. If you want to file an age discrimination charge, you may file it either with the EEOC or with a state or local agency that is authorized to receive them and to enforce relevant state laws.

Figuring out where to file a charge can be difficult. You may do so either in writing or by telephone. You may want to file directly with the EEOC in Washington or, if there is one locat-

Cash Balance Plans

In recent years, numerous companies have created a new type of retirement plan called a cash balance plan. Many employees whose companies have replaced other pension plans with cash balance plans claim that the new plans discriminate against mid-career and/or older workers. The Equal Employment Opportunity Commission created a team to study whether these plans are discriminatory, but at press time there had been no official ruling.

For more information on cash balance plans, see page 44 in Chapter Two.

ed near you, at an EEOC regional office. Call the agency's toll-free number, 1-800-669-4000, to connect with the office closest to your home. The EEOC also has agreements that allow many state or local agencies to pursue the charges filed under the federal law, so you may end up being referred to one of these.

In any case, you will be asked to provide:

• Basic information, including your name, address, and phone number, and the name and address of the person whom you are charging with the violation;

• "A clear and concise statement of the facts" of the discrimination you are alleging;

• If you know it, the approximate number of employees of the employer or labor organization you are naming in the charge; and

• A statement saying whether charges have also been filed with a state agency and if so, the name of the agency and date of the filing.

Timing for filing a charge can be crucial. If you live in a state with an age discrimination law, you can wait up to 300 days after the discriminatory event—for example, after you were turned down for a promotion, or when you were pressured into early retirement—to file the charge. State laws generally require you to file within 180 days. If your state does not have a law, you must file with the EEOC within 180 days.

You will probably want to talk with a lawyer before deciding exactly how and when to proceed with filing a discrimination charge. We'll discuss this in more detail on page 97.

After receiving the charge, the EEOC interviews you about the situation, notifies your employer that the charge has been filed, and investigates the facts to determine if you appear to have a case under the law. If you do, the agency will work with you and your employer to try to achieve an out-of-court settlement or other resolution to the disagreement.

Remedies for Age Discrimination

If you take an age discrimination case to court and win, you could receive back wages and fringe benefits you have lost up until the trial, attorney's fees and costs, and possible reinstatement in your job. If reinstatement is not an option, the judge may also award you "front pay," which consists of the salary and fringe benefits you would have received in the future had you not been discriminated against. In some states, you may also be awarded punitive or compensatory damages.

DECISIONS YOU NEED TO MAKE ABOUT JOB PROTECTION

ARE YOU BEING DISCRIMINATED AGAINST BECAUSE OF YOUR AGE?

How can you tell whether your employer is breaking the law, or simply making prudent decisions that will improve the company's bottom line? The first decision you need to make is whether you have evidence that your employer is breaking the law.

Experts in the field point to two types of clues to discrimination—obvious clues and more subtle ones. Obvious clues include comments from management, such as "we need some

Warning Signs of Age Discrimination in Employment

Here are some of the most tell-tale signs of age discrimination:

1. Your employer lays off older employees, saying the company needs to downsize. Soon afterwards, you notice that the company has placed classified ads looking for people to fill the same positions that have just been vacated.

2. Your job responsibilities and functions suddenly change. For example, you are shifted from a position of supervising one hundred people to supervising only three. Or you are asked to perform an extremely difficult task, such as opening up a sales territory that no one else has been able to crack.

3. The atmosphere in your office changes. You're a long-term employee. Suddenly your boss seems to be criticizing everything you do, or even humiliating you publicly.

4. Your performance ratings take a dive, even though you believe you are doing your job as well as or better than in the past.

new blood around here," or "younger employees are more energetic." Downsizing a fifty-year-old employee and immediately replacing him or her with a thirty-five-year-old who makes $20,000 less per year may also be an obvious clue.

However, according to L. Steven Platt, a Chicago lawyer who specializes in age discrimination cases, many employers use more subtle methods, including calculated deception, when they want to force an employee to retire because of his or her age. "It takes a really perceptive person to be able to spot the signs," says Platt. "The person affected can spot them in retrospect, and I can spot them as an outsider. But people who go through it tend not to see it coming. . . . Most of the people I deal with have been dramatically misled for a long period of time."

For example, Platt says, a company may assign an older employee to a new position where he has less responsibility than in his current job. "Then management writes an internal memo telling employees that this person has a great new career opportunity, because it doesn't want to demoralize people while pushing them out the door. People may be moved around into other positions over a long period of time, and not dealt with honestly."

SHOULD YOU TRY TO NEGOTIATE DIRECTLY WITH YOUR EMPLOYER?

Your options for fighting age discrimination range from trying to resolve the issue yourself, at your workplace, to filing formal charges, and, if an agreement cannot be worked out, ultimately taking your employer to court.

The AARP, which provides information about this problem and serves as an advocate for older employees, suggests that you consider trying to negotiate with your employer. One way to do this may be through the company's complaint or grievance procedure, which may be governed by a union contract. Another would be to talk directly with your supervisor about your situation.

Before negotiating, however, AARP suggests that you learn as much as you can about the financial status and the practices of the company, as well as about factors that may affect your own case. The AARP also suggests that you try to get answers to some questions before you make your first move to challenge an action you believe discriminates against you on the basis of age:

Is the company in good financial shape? Are the layoffs really necessary? What exactly are the company's personnel policies? Is the company following the policies? Is the company recruiting younger employees at the same time it is laying off older ones? Are training opportunities only being offered to younger employees? Are other employees being laid off or denied their full pension benefits?

The answers you find to these questions may help you decide whether you should try to negotiate with the company or pursue other options.

SHOULD YOU HIRE A LAWYER?

Platt suggests that you consult a lawyer as soon as you suspect that you're being discriminated against. If the issue is a job termination or early retirement, he says, you should talk to a lawyer while you are still on the job. "You have more leverage than when you are terminated," Platt explains. Often, if a person has already consulted with a lawyer, the company may agree to a better separation agreement than you would otherwise receive.

The catch, of course, is that hiring a lawyer costs money. "Most specialists may do an initial consultation for free or for a reduced rate," says former AARP attorney Cathy Ventrell-Monsees. "The fee is well worth the advice you'll get, because, usually in an hour, an experienced employment attorney can tell whether you are likely to have a chance of winning your case," she says.

A lawyer can either help you negotiate with your employer or, if you have already left the job or if negotiations fail, outline your other options. A key decision will be whether to pursue your charge in a state court or on the federal level, and you'll need legal advice on which route would give you the best shot at winning. The answer will depend on several factors, including previous decisions of the state or federal courts on employment issues, how long it's likely to take to resolve the case, and the types of remedies available to you. In some states, you may be able to collect punitive and/or compensatory damage awards; in others you may not.

The rates charged by lawyers differ depending on where you live. If you are lucky, you might find a lawyer willing to take the case on a contingency basis, meaning you would only pay if you won the case. In a big city, Ventrell-Monsees says, you may have to pay a retainer of $5,000 or $10,000 to get the case moving, as well as pay expenses such as fees for copying and filing court papers. If you win your case, the court may also award payment of your attorney's fees.

WHAT FACTORS SHOULD YOU CONSIDER IN DECIDING WHETHER TO FIGHT AGE DISCRIMINATION?

A commitment to a legal fight will tax the financial and psychological resources of both you and your family. Even if you preserve your job, the legal protection you have against retaliation cannot shield you from the likelihood of increased anxiety and stress. If you leave your job, you'll have to look for another one that pays as well, or live on other financial resources.

Ventrell-Monsees estimates that the average amount of time required to resolve an age discrimination case in the courts is five years. The time could vary widely, of course, depending on the backlog in the court where you have filed. Platt says that in Chicago it could take anywhere from nine months to five years.

Furthermore, the record of what happens to cases filed with the EEOC is not encouraging. In 1999, the EEOC received 14,141 charges of age discrimination, adding to a huge backlog of many types of cases, including discrimination against people with disabilities, sexual harassment, and other charges of civil rights violations.

In 1996 the EEOC "resolved" more than 15,448 cases, but the agency only took twelve age discrimination lawsuits to court. Of the cases resolved, only 17 percent resulted, through settlement or conciliation or other processes, in an outcome that favored the employee. EEOC found that nearly two-thirds of the charges filed had no basis, and another one-quarter were withdrawn for "administrative" reasons, such as being unable to locate the person who filed the charge, or as a result of other court decisions that made it "futile" to pursue the case.

This is not to say that you shouldn't take on a legal fight—only to urge you to consider the decision thoroughly before making a commitment. Here are some of the questions you

Success Story: Fighting Age Discrimination in the Courts

Despite the discouraging data on resolution of age discrimination cases by the federal Equal Employment Opportunity Commission (see page 98), you should know that some people who take their cases to court do win, and are well rewarded for their trouble.

Steve Platt, an employment lawyer in Chicago, relates this true story of a man we'll call Joe, a forty-seven-and-a-half-year-old shift manager for a manufacturing company in a Midwestern state. When Joe and other workers refused an early retirement package offered by their employer, the company came down hard on them, supervising them closely and changing their shifts frequently—so frequently that the workers became physically ill. Finally the company terminated Joe, charging poor job performance, despite clear evidence that his unit was contributing much more than its share of the plant's profits.

Joe sued the company for age discrimination, and the legal fight took five years. He'd spent his entire career in manufacturing, and at his age he couldn't get another good job in his field. For years he struggled financially, first trying to sell real estate and then starting a small family printing business.

When the case finally went to trial, the company literally had some ten lawyers in the courtroom, but Joe won anyway. The settlement was $1.2 million. He was compensated for loss of wages and reinstated in his old job. Most importantly, he gained the right to a better pension, because the company's pension plan provided much higher retirement benefits to people who did not retire until after they were fifty years old.

should ask yourself and discuss with your family and/or a financial advisor:

1. How old are you, and how many years do you want to continue working before you retire? The older you are, the harder it will be to find a job that you want, at the salary you need.

2. If the case involves involuntary retirement: Do you have enough financial resources to retire now? For example, will you need to pay college expenses for your children in the next few years? Will your retirement income cover the mortgage payments and expenses of maintaining the family home?

3. Are you psychologically prepared to stop working? How would early retirement affect plans you and your spouse may have made?

4. Do you want to continue to work for your employer if you have the opportunity? If the case involves an issue that would not require you to leave, such as discrimination in promotion or pay or benefits, will you be able to withstand the potential tension at work if you stay with the company after filing a charge?

5. If you win a lawsuit, does the company have the financial means to pay up?

6. What will it cost you to pursue legal action? Can you afford to lose?

7. Do you have the psychological resources to withstand a contentious procedure that could continue for several years?

Once you have discussed and analyzed these factors, you will be ready to decide whether to try to negotiate with your employer, accept some type of settlement, or pursue your case in the courts.

THE TAX FACTOR

There are two ways that becoming involved in an age discrimination action could ultimately affect your tax status: if you end up taking early retirement or if you win your case and receive a financial settlement.

Early Retirement

The effect that early retirement will have on your tax bill depends on these related factors: your age, whether you decide to continue working after retiring from your current job, and the type of pension or retirement savings you have.

If you have a defined benefit pension plan that guarantees you a regular payment—for example, $1,000 per month—you must pay ordinary income taxes on that amount from the time that you start receiving the pension. If you take another job or work for yourself, you'll pay income tax both on your earnings from the new job or business and on the pension.

If you have a 401(k) or other retirement savings plan, you'll pay a penalty if you withdraw the money before you are fifty-nine and a half years old—this is known as a "lump-sum distribution." Specifically, you will have to pay a 20 percent withholding tax on the pre-tax contributions, plus a 10 percent penalty or "early distribution" tax. There are three ways to avoid these taxes:

• If your employer permits it, and you want to, you may keep the money in the 401(k) at the company until you turn fifty-nine and a half;

• If you take a job with a different employer and if it is permitted, you may "roll over" the money from your previous employer's 401(k) and put it into an account with your new employer; or

• You may withdraw the 401(k) money in a lump sum and deposit it directly into an Individual Retirement Account. This type of rollover will help you avoid penalties only if you follow some very strict rules for doing it. Be sure to check with a financial advisor before taking action. (See Chapter Two for a discussion of this strategy.)

The date you choose to retire can make a big difference both in your retirement income and in your psychological health. Attractive as early retirement may sound, for many people it will not work financially. Leaving a job before your pension is vested or being required to withdraw your retirement savings in a lump sum may seriously undermine what you thought was the financial security you'd planned on for your golden years. Equally unappealing, when you feel vigorous and motivated to continue working, is being told that you must leave your job because your employer does not value your work anymore.

That's why it is against the law to reduce benefits, fire, or force someone into early retirement simply on the basis of age. If your employer makes an early retirement offer or changes your job status or benefits, you should take the following steps to protect yourself against possible age discrimination:

• Analyze any changes occurring in the company, such as hiring younger employees, to see if there are signs your employer is practicing age discrimination;

• If you are asked to sign a waiver in return for accepting an early retirement package, make sure that your employer is following all of the legal requirements; and

• If you believe you are being discriminated against, consult an expert in employment law about your options for arriving at a negotiated settlement, as well as what is involved in initiating legal action.

FOR MORE INFORMATION

BY TELEPHONE

AARP

Call 1-800-424-3410 to request a free copy of "Employment Discrimination Against Midlife and Older Women—Vol. 1: How Courts Treat Sex-and-Age Discrimination Cases" (D16262) and to request any other current AARP publications on age discrimination in employment. For help in locating employment lawyers in your state, call AARP's Litigation Department at 202-434-2060.

Equal Employment Opportunity Commission (EEOC)

If you do not find an EEOC office listed in "United States Government" section of your local phone book, call 1-800-669-4000 or 1-800-669-6820 (TDD) to locate the one closest to you.

BY MAIL

EEOC

To order a free fact sheet, "Facts About Age Discrimination," write to EEOC's Office of Communications and Legislative Affairs, 1801 L St. N.W., Room 9405, Washington, DC 20507.

National Academy of Elder Law Attorneys (NAELA)

You may order a brochure, "Questions & Answers When Looking for an Elder Law Attorney," by sending a self-addressed, stamped legal-size envelope to NAELA at 1604 North Country Club Road, Tucson, AZ 85716 and enclosing $2.25.

National Employment Lawyers Association (NELA)

For a list of lawyers who specialize in the field, write them at 600 Harrison St., Suite 535, San Francisco, CA 94107, and enclose a self-addressed, stamped, letter-size envelope. NELA will not accept fax or telephone requests.

ON THE INTERNET

Use these addresses to look for information on age discrimination in employment and/or find a lawyer:

www.aoa.gov/factsheet/ageism.html
This is a good general summary of the issue.

www.aarp.org
From the home page, you can choose "Legal Resources," then "Whom Do I Call? Where do I Go?" Click on "Administration on Aging" to see a state-by-state list—with addresses and phone and fax numbers—of agencies on aging. They offer information on legal assistance providers and hotlines. Choose "Getting Answers" at the home page to see "The AARP Guide to Internet Resources Related to Aging." Sites are listed by subject, such as government, health, and law.

www.eeoc.gov
This site provides a wealth of detailed information about age discrimination, including the EEOC fact sheet mentioned above, instructions on how to file a charge, and the text of relevant laws and regulations.

www.naela.org
The website of the National Academy of Elder Law Attorneys allows you to order brochures on age discrimination and other elder law issues from the website.

www.legal.net
For a state-by-state list of lawyers specializing in employment or civil rights law, click on the "Attorneys Registry."

PART TWO

PROMOTING AND MAINTAINING YOUR HEALTH

CHAPTER FIVE

Medicare — The Good News and the Bad

Tom's arthritis was getting bad, so he decided to take early retirement and start collecting Social Security at age sixty-two. He figured out his expenses, including a payment for the Part B Medicare premium to cover visits to the doctor and some other medical expenses, and decided he could afford to retire.

When he went to the Social Security office to enroll, however, Tom was shocked to learn that Medicare coverage does not start until age sixty-five. If he retired at sixty-two, he would have to pay $4,000 a year for health insurance out of his limited retirement budget.

WHAT YOU NEED TO KNOW ABOUT MEDICARE BENEFITS

Medicare was created in 1965 to meet the needs of people as they grow older, when they are no longer working and do not get health insurance as an employment benefit.

We've all heard of Medicare, but figuring out what it means to you when you retire is another story. Does everyone automatically qualify for Medicare? Does Medicare pay for all of your health care when you retire? What services does Medicare provide? What are your rights as a consumer? "When people on Medicare become ill they often have no idea what the costs to them will be," says Andrew Laurenson, a social worker in Martinsburg, WV. For example, he said, "They have no idea what the copayments will be, or that they will have to pay for

Can You Count on Medicare?

Medicare, like Social Security, faces a financial crisis. For several years in the late 1990s, it appeared that a Medicare financial crisis was imminent: that a shortfall in funding hospital costs would occur as soon as the year 2001. To respond to the dire predictions, in 1997 Congress passed and the President signed a bill that they hoped would stave off the crisis.

In the April 2000 Medicare Trustees report, however, there was much better news: The Trustees estimated that the Medicare hospital fund could in fact remain solvent until 2025. Whether that prediction will be fulfilled is hard to say. For one thing, in 2010 the first baby boomers will become eligible for Medicare, and in future years the number of people the program will have to serve will continue to grow.

Moreover, the Medicare fund undoubtedly benefited from the increased taxes paid into it during the booming economy of the late 1990s. The level of future tax support will of course depend on how the economy fares.

For several years policymakers have been debating how they could shore up the Medicare program to meet its future needs. Among the solutions that have been proposed are:

• Raising the payroll tax that you must pay as long as you are working. In 2001 you only pay your tax (FICA) on $80,400 of earned income. This amount increases automatically each year, and if Congress wanted to raise it substantially, this could be done.

• Further increasing the Part B premium, the amount that Medicare beneficiaries pay every month to cover expenses for physicians and related services. In 2001, the premium is $50.00 per month.

• Hiking the eligibility age for Medicare, from the current sixty-five, possibly to sixty-seven, over a decade or more.

If you're worried about the Medicare shortfall, just remember this: Medicare is one of the government's most popular programs, with one of the strongest lobbies in Washington. The politicians who need these voters to get elected are unlikely to take any action that would strand many of their constituents without adequate medical coverage.

their medications." Unless you know how Medicare works, you can end up spending more than you'd planned on health care, and having to cut back on other retirement expenses.

This chapter gives you basic information on what the program is and what it does—information that you need to know to make plans for your retirement, and to make choices about the type of health care you'll receive. If you are already retired and on Medicare, you may learn some things about the program that you didn't know.

What this chapter does not try to do, however, is give you all the details on filing claims and working your way through the Medicare system. For help with your own claims or other issues, you should contact one of the organizations listed at the end of this chapter in the "resources" section of "For Your Information."

The following section provides you with the most current information on key Medicare issues, including eligibility, how to enroll and the cost and benefits of Medicare.

WHO IS ELIGIBLE FOR MEDICARE?

You are eligible for Medicare if you are sixty-five and:

• You worked at least ten years in covered employment, the same as for Social Security; or

• You're entitled to Social Security benefits based on your husband's or wife's work record, or your ex-spouse's work record, and the spouse is at least sixty-two; or

• If you worked long enough in a federal, state, or local government job to be insured for Medicare.

(Note: There are some exceptions to the "age sixty-five" eligibility rule. They include people who have been on Social Security disability benefits for at least two years, and those with end-stage renal disease who require kidney dialysis or transplants.)

The crucial point you need to know for retirement planning is the one that Tom, in the example above, learned the hard way: You may retire and start to collect Social Security at sixty-two. But you may not start on Medicare until you are sixty-five. If you retire at sixty-two, it's possible that you'll continue to receive health insurance coverage through your employer—probably paying an expensive premium—but probably only for another eighteen months. (The federal law that ensures this extension—known as COBRA—is described in Chapter Seven.) And if you are self-employed, you're probably already struggling to find affordable coverage, which gets more expensive as you get older. If you retire earlier, you'll have to search for health insurance on the open market until you're sixty-five. (See Chapter Seven for tips on how to find other health coverage.)

HOW DO I SIGN UP FOR MEDICARE?

If you are already receiving Social Security (a majority of Americans start before they are sixty-five) Uncle Sam will automatically mail you a Medicare enrollment card three months before you turn sixty-five. People who are not receiving Social Security or Railroad Retirement (a special federal program for railway workers and their families) should apply for Medicare by contacting any Social Security office (or, if you or your spouse worked for a railroad, the Railroad Retirement Board), three months before you turn sixty-five.

If you don't enroll in Medicare within seven months of turning sixty-five, you'll have to wait for a "general enrollment period," between the next January 1 and March 31, to start your coverage the July 1 after that.

You may recall that to qualify for Social Security, you must have worked the equivalent of ten years (forty quarters or forty periods of three months each) in covered employment, paying into the system through the payroll tax. Part of this tax goes to support the Medicare system.

Medicare offers people who are sixty-five two main types of coverage. Part A pays the bills for expenses incurred while you are in the hospital, as well as for skilled nursing facilities, home health services, and hospice care. Part B covers outpatient hospital expenses, doctors' bills, medical equipment and supplies, and services such as lab tests.

Sign Up for Medicare Part B as Soon as You Can

If you don't sign up promptly, you could end up paying more for your Medicare for the rest of your life! Here's what can happen:

Medicare offers people who are sixty-five two main types of coverage—Part A, which pays the bills incurred when you are in the hospital, and Part B, which covers doctor bills and certain other medical services such as lab tests.

Everyone who signs up for Part B must pay a monthly premium. If you enroll in Part B during the seven-month enrollment period that starts three months before the month you turn sixty-five, you'll pay the regular premium: $50.00 in 2001.

But if you delay your enrollment to the annual "general enrollment" period, from January 1 to March 31, you will pay a higher rate for the Part B premium, *for the rest of your life*. The amount of the increase will be 10 percent for every year that you delay signing up. (If you continue working after you turn sixty-five, and do not enroll in Medicare until you leave your job and lose the health insurance your employer provides, this penalty does not apply.)

If you have qualified for Social Security by working and contributing to the system for ten years, you will receive Medicare Part A coverage automatically. But if you did not work the ten years and want the coverage, you must pay a premium, just as you would for any other health insurance. In 2001, the premium is $300 per month if you have worked and paid into the system for seven and a half years (thirty quarters) or less, and $165 per month if you have worked and paid into the system for thirty to forty quarters.

If you do not qualify for automatic Part A coverage and want to have it, you should sign up within the seven-month period that starts three months before you turn sixty-five. If you delay longer, you will have to pay a penalty of 10 percent in addition to the premium.

WHAT DOES MEDICARE COST?

As explained above, for the hospital services provided under Part A, most people do not pay an out-of-pocket premium. However, under Medicare, just as in other health insurance programs, you must pay some copayments and deductibles. (See page 115 for details.)

For the non-hospital services, such as lab tests, which you receive under Part B, you must pay a monthly premium—$50 in 2001—which is automatically deducted from your Social Security benefit. The amount of the premium is adjusted annually. Part B also has a $100 annual deductible, which means that in each calendar year you will have to pay out of pocket for the first $100 worth of services you receive.

You may get insurance coverage for services that Medicare does not provide by purchasing a Medicare supplemental or Medigap insurance policy, the cost of which can range anywhere from slightly over $300 to more than $2,000 per year.

WHAT ASSISTANCE CAN I GET IN PAYING MY MEDICARE BILLS?

People whose income is at or near the poverty level, and who have no more than $4,000 in assets for an individual, or $6,000 for a married couple, may qualify for assistance in paying some Medicare fees. There are three programs that may be able to help—each with different financial requirements and benefits. They're called, respectively, the Qualified Medicare Beneficiary (QMB) program, the Specified Low-Income Medicare Beneficiary (SLMB) program, and the Qualifying Individual (QI) program. The types of expenses that may be covered through these programs include deductibles and coinsurance for hospital stays, and the Part B monthly premium and deductibles. If you think that you or someone you know might qualify, contact your local Social Security office or local medical assistance office for more information. You can locate these offices by calling the Medicare toll-free number, 1-800-633-4227. If you call the Medicare number, also ask them to send you a copy of a brochure, "Medicare Savings for Qualified Beneficiaries," which provides basic information on these programs. You may read the same brochure on the Internet at www.medicare.gov.

WHAT TYPES OF HEALTH CARE PROGRAMS ARE AVAILABLE TO ME UNDER MEDICARE?

There are three ways to receive your Medicare services: the "original Medicare plan," also known as "fee-for-service"; Medicare managed care; or "private fee-for-service." Another option is a "medical savings account." Here's a brief description of how each of these works.

"Original Medicare" or Fee-for-Service

You choose your own doctor and other providers. Medicare pays them for the services they provide to you according to a schedule of approved fees. As long as your doctor "accepts Medicare assignment," as the jargon goes, Uncle Sam pays 80 percent of the cost based on a government scale and you pay the other 20 percent. If you go to a doctor who is not in Medicare, you generally end up paying 15 percent more. With this option you will not have coverage for most prescription drugs, hearing aids, or vision care.

Medicare Managed Care

This option is also sometimes called "Medicare + Choice." You join a plan that provides and supervises all of your care for a set fee—generally less than you would pay for the same service under the traditional Medicare—it receives each year from Medicare. Generally, you are only covered for care from doctors and other providers who are in the HMO and its network. HMOs may charge a small premium or copayment, but generally they cost less than the traditional fee-for-service Medicare. They also tend to offer more routine and preventive care—in some cases, this includes partial coverage for prescription drugs.

Some managed care plans offer a "Point of Service" option, which allows you to receive services from doctors and hospitals that are not in the plan. You usually pay an extra fee for this benefit.

Private Fee-for-Service

This option allows Medicare clients to buy an insurance policy that offers benefits beyond those required by Medicare. You may use any doctor or hospital that accepts the plan's payment. However, Medicare does not limit the cost of premiums, so this option can be quite expensive.

Medical Savings Accounts

MSAs are accounts, similar to an IRA, where you can save money on a tax-deferred basis to be spent later for medical care. Although this program is on the books, it has not been popular and was unavailable at the time this book was written. To get an idea of how a medicare MSA might work, read the description starting on page 170 in Chapter Seven.

WHAT SERVICES ARE COVERED BY MEDICARE?

It would be nice to think that once you are on Medicare, you'll never have to pay another medical bill. Unfortunately, that's not true. "People think that Medicare is going to cover everything, and it doesn't," comments Lynne Meyer, whose company, Medical Business Associates, helps Medicare patients get their bills paid. For example, she says, a person may be allergic to the dye used in a certain medical test, so the doctor will order a different test. The first test would have been covered by Medicare, but the test that is actually performed is not. When the bill arrives, the patient is shocked to find that Medicare won't pay it.

This example shows why you should always ask your doctor, or the person who handles insurance in the doctor's office, whether the recommended service or procedure is actually covered or if you'll have to pay for it personally.

Here are some of the costs that Medicare *doesn't* cover:

Long-term or Custodial Care
The federal program that pays for most nursing home care is Medicaid. (See Chapter Six for more information on Uncle Sam's role in paying for nursing care.)

In the Hospital
Extra cost of a private room or private-duty nurse (unless your doctor says it is necessary for medical reasons), and personal conveniences such as a television or telephone.

Out of the Hospital
Many routine and preventive services, such as physicals, dental care, eye exams, and eyeglasses. (However, if you are in a managed care program, some of these may be included.)

Prescriptions
Medicare does not pay for prescription drugs that you take when you are not in the hospital. (An exception is made for oral chemotherapy drugs and drugs that must be administered by a doctor.) Medicare HMOs usually offer some prescription coverage, but the type of coverage and amount of drugs covered varies widely.

WHAT SERVICES DOES MEDICARE PART A COVER?
This part of Medicare pays expenses associated with a stay in the hospital, continued treatment or rehabilitation in a skilled nursing facility, some home health services, and hospice care for the terminally ill. In some cases, you must pay a deductible or coinsurance. Here are the basic Part A services, along with the charges you must pay for these services in 2001 (the fees usually go up annually):

Hospitalization

In 2001, Medicare pays for a semiprivate room and board, general nursing, and other hospital services and supplies:

- First 60 days: All but a deductible of $792
- 61st to 90th day: You must pay $198 per day
- 91st to 150th day: You must pay $396 per day
- Beyond 150 days: You must pay entire bill
- 60 lifetime reserve days: These are days in the hospital, beyond the limits described above, which you may receive coverage for if you need them to pay your bill. For these days, you pay coinsurance of $396 in 2001.

All of these amounts tend to go up a few dollars each year.

Skilled Nursing Facility Care

Medicare pays only if a hospital discharges you to a skilled nursing facility (SNF) after a stay of at least three days. An SNF offers skilled nursing care and rehabilitation, but it is not the same as a nursing home, which primarily offers custodial and personal care. Medicare will pay if you require skilled nursing and rehabilitation, but if the main expenses of your stay are custodial services such as assistance in bathing and walking, Medicare will not pay for them.

Medicare covers the cost of a semiprivate room and board, skilled nursing and rehabilitative services, and other services and supplies:

First 20 days: Medicare pays 100 percent
Additional 80 days: You pay up to $99 per day
Beyond 100 days: Medicare pays nothing.

Home Health Care

Part A covers the first one hundred days of home care after a three-day stay in a hospital or skilled nursing facility. After that, you may have the costs covered under Part B. To receive home health care, you must be homebound and require intermittent skilled nursing care, physical therapy, or speech language therapy. Your doctor must certify that you need the care, and must make a plan that describes the types of services you need and the frequency. The services must be provided by an agency that is approved by Medicare.

Hospice Care

Medicare pays for hospice care for a person who is certified terminally ill by a doctor, and who chooses to receive hospice care instead of the standard Medicare benefits for the illness. To continue to receive hospice care after ninety days, the patient must be recertified every sixty days. Except for a possible copayment of up to $5 each for drug prescriptions and 5 percent of Medicare's approved daily rate for respite care—allowing temporary relief to persons who assist with home care—Medicare pays all costs.

Blood

If you require blood transfusions while in a hospital or skilled nursing facility, you must pay for the first three pints per calendar year. Medicare covers the rest.

WHAT SERVICES DOES PART B COVER?

This part of Medicare covers your doctor bills and a wide range of other medical expenses—clinical laboratory services, home health care, outpatient hospital treatment, blood, and ambulatory surgical services. The key difference from Part A is that in most cases, Medicare pays 80 percent of the approved cost of Part B services, and you must pay the other 20 percent plus a $100 annual deductible. Here's a summary of the services and what they may cost you:

Medical Expenses

This includes doctor's bills, inpatient and outpatient medical and surgical services, outpatient supplies, physical and speech therapy, diagnostic tests, and other services such as flu shots, Pap smears, and ambulance costs. Coverage is unlimited if the service is medically necessary. Medicare pays 80 percent of the approved cost for each service; you pay 20 percent. For outpatient mental health services, Medicare generally pays only 50 percent.

Clinical Laboratory Services
For urinalyses, blood tests, etc., Medicare generally pays 100 percent.

Home Health Care
Coverage for this is now split between Parts A and B of Medicare. For people who do not have Part A, all home health care is covered under Part B, as long as the conditions described above are met. Between 1998 and 2003, the government will be phasing some of the coverage now offered under Part A into Part B.

Blood
If you need blood when you are not receiving Part A benefits in a hospital or skilled nursing facility, you'll pay for the first three pints, plus 20 percent of the remaining cost after your Part B deductible is paid.

Ambulatory Surgical Services
For procedures that don't require a hospital stay, Medicare covers 80 percent.

WHAT KIND OF PREVENTIVE HEALTH BENEFITS DOES MEDICARE OFFER?
In recent years Medicare has expanded the types of preventive benefits available and broadened eligibility for them. In some cases, these benefits are available to all Medicare clients and in others, only to people who are at high risk for a particular disease. These include mammograms, Pap smears, and pelvic exams; screening for prostate cancer, colorectal cancer, and diabetes; and measurement of bone mass if there is a risk of osteoporosis. If you're in an HMO, the benefits may include other preventive measures such as routine physicals.

CAN I GET ADDITIONAL HEALTH INSURANCE TO PAY FOR THE SERVICES MEDICARE DOES NOT COVER?

Jack, sixty-seven, and Mary, sixty-six, were both on Medicare fee-for-service in their home city of Chicago, when they decided that they wanted to escape from the severe winter by spending two months traveling in Mexico. One day Jack had chest pains and was admitted to a hospital in Mexico City. He did not require surgery, but the bill for several days in the hospital, plus diagnostic tests, was $12,000. Jack submitted the bill to Medicare, and was shocked to learn that Medicare does not cover health care costs if you are outside the U.S. Jack had no alternative but to pay the bill out of his retirement savings.

If Jack had known about Medigap—a type of insurance policy that covers expenses that Medicare does not pay—he could have bought a policy for an annual premium of about $1,000 and saved himself $11,000 that year.

People who are lucky enough to have retirement health insurance benefits from their previous employer or who join an HMO may find that these fill the coverage gaps that exist in Medicare. About one-third of people on Medicare, however, purchase a supplemental policy, referred to as Medigap, from an insurance company. This pays expenses such as the coinsurance and deductible on a hospital stay (see description of Part A benefits above), the Part B premium and deductible emergency medical costs during foreign travel, and/or prescription drugs. When you turn sixty-five, you have six months to sign up for Medigap. Once you are enrolled, you cannot be denied a policy because of your age or health condition. But if you don't sign up during those six months, an insurer has a right to turn down your application. Some states, however, have a more generous enrollment requirement. Check with your state's insurance department to find out what rules apply to you.

The government approves ten standard Medigap policies that private insurance companies may sell to you. The most basic benefit package, called Plan A, essentially covers the coinsurance charges you would otherwise have to pay under Medicare Part A

Medigap Plan A

The ten government-approved Medigap plans must include the following benefits. If you buy only Plan A, these are the only Medigap benefits you will have:

 • The Part A coinsurance required for the 61st through 90th day of hospitalization;

 • Coinsurance for your sixty "lifetime reserve" days in the hospital;

 • Full coverage for an additional 365 days in the hospital;

 • The cost of the first three pints of blood per year that are not paid for by Part A or Part B; and

 • Coinsurance for Part B charges, usually 20 percent (50 percent for mental health benefits), after you have paid the annual $100 deductible.

or Part B. However, the government has recently approved the offering of two new versions of Medigap plans with a high deductible. These are labeled Plan F and Plan J with a $1,500 deductible, compared to the ten policies that have no deductible.

Medigap plans B through J offer a mix-and-match selection of coverage including: coinsurance for skilled nursing care, the Part A or Part B deductibles, emergency coverage while you're traveling abroad, and prescription drugs. For charts and details on what the ten Medigap plans cover, see the "Guide to Health Insurance for People with Medicare," published by the National Association of Insurance Commissioners and the Health Care Financing Administration. You can order a free copy by calling the Medicare Hotline, 1-800-633-4227.

The premiums and deductibles on these policies can vary tremendously, depending on where you live, as well as the benefits included and your age. Not all of the policies are offered for sale in every state, so you may have fewer than ten from which to choose. A Washington, D.C., advocacy group, Families USA, has released

"The Crushing Costs of Medicare Supplemental Policies," a study of the Medigap premiums charged by Prudential and Blue Cross Blue Shield, which in 1995 and 1996 represented more than 50 percent of the national market.

The study found that the cost of an identical Plan A policy—which includes the required Medigap "basic benefits," purchased in 1996, was $311 per year in New Mexico, $325 in Kansas, $825 in New Jersey, and $876 in Ohio.

The Medigap Plan J policy is the most comprehensive, including coverage for emergencies when you are traveling overseas, costs of recuperating from an illness at home, and up to $3,000 in extra coverage for drugs. Families USA reported that the cost of this type of policy ranged from $1,332 per year in Arkansas to $2,205 in California.

WHAT ARE MY RIGHTS AS A MEDICARE PATIENT?

The government has very detailed rules that ensure you certain legal rights. Patients who feel that any of these rights are being denied them should use the appeals process to challenge decisions by Medicare providers. The process is bureaucratic and complex, but you can get help if you contact one of the Medicare support organizations listed in the "For Your Information" at the end of this chapter.

1. The right to confidentiality.

Your Medicare provider is required to establish safeguards for your medical records to ensure the privacy of any "individually identifiable" information. Health care professionals and insurance carriers are allowed to have access to your medical records if they need it for your care, but otherwise your records are supposed to be confidential. This means, for example, that government officials do not have access to them.

2. The right to choose the type of Medicare program or provider that suits you best.

This right places a burden on you to figure out whether the traditional fee-for-service, HMO, or another Medicare health insurance option will be the most convenient, affordable, and effective.

3. The right to change your Medicare health insurance option.

Although there are some exceptions and there can be financial disadvantages to shifting from, for example, an HMO to a fee-for-service plan, you do have a right to make the change.

Here's an example, provided by the Medicare Rights Center, a nonprofit advocacy organization in New York, of a reason for changing your Medicare provider. Mr. K had a problem with an irregular heartbeat, and his fee-for-service doctor told him his heart should be tested twice a year. Mr. K joined an HMO and only found out afterward that unless he became very ill, the HMO would only pay for the test once a year. Mr. K left the HMO and returned to his original doctor.

4. The right to medically necessary care.

This entitles you to receive the care that is generally the custom of the medical profession for your diagnosis. The decision must be made on a case-by-case basis. If a treatment is not considered "medically necessary," it is generally termed "experimental." You should keep in mind, however, that the same treatment may be considered medically necessary by one provider and experimental by another. For example, intensive chemotherapy for breast cancer is considered experimental in many states, but in New York it is considered necessary in certain cases.

5. The right to a second or third opinion about your medical treatment.

This issue arises most often when surgery is being proposed, but may also arise in other cases, such as whether it is more appropriate to treat a cancer with chemotherapy or radiation.

If you question your doctor's medical recommendation, Medicare will pay for you to get a second opinion as long as the condition is covered by Medicare. If the first two doctors do not agree, Medicare will pay for you to get a third opinion. If you're in an HMO, Medicare will pay the fee of a second doctor within the network. But if you go to a doctor outside the network, you will have to pay the bill. If the two doctors you have consulted do not agree, Medicare will pay for a third opinion.

6. The right to be told about all treatment options that may be appropriate for your condition, regardless of their cost.
In the past, Medicare was severely criticized for allowing participating HMOs, as a cost-cutting measure, to tell patients only about the *least expensive* therapies for their condition. Under a law passed in 1997, patients have a right to be informed about *all* of the options. If you don't want to accept the option that is proposed, you may appeal the decision, as explained below.

7. If you have an HMO: The right to expedited reconsideration of denial of treatment or coverage.
Medicare normally allows your HMO to take sixty days to decide whether you require a particular service or treatment.

However, if you have an urgent medical condition and you are denied treatment, you or your doctor may ask the HMO to reconsider that decision and respond within seventy-two hours. Having your doctor, rather than you personally, make the request will ensure that the decision is expedited.

The HMO is supposed to expedite the appeal if waiting sixty days for a decision would threaten your life, your health, or your ability to regain maximum function. The third condition refers to a situation in which you believe you need immediate therapy to insure that you will regain normal use, for example, of a broken limb.

If your request for the service or treatment is rejected, Medicare also has procedures for filing a grievance or an appeal.

8. The right to appeal a denial of Medicare coverage.
If Medicare refuses to pay the bill for a service you believe should be covered, you may appeal the decision. For disputes that involve $100 or more, the process, called a fair hearing, is informal and may not even require you to be present. For a dispute that involves $500 or more, you may request a hearing

before an Administrative Law Judge of the Social Security Administration.

Consider this true story provided by the Medicare Rights Center. After a hip replacement, Mrs. M. was referred by her HMO doctor to a skilled nursing facility (SNF) for rehabilitation. The HMO said that she would only benefit from three weeks of care, and that's all they would pay for. However, both Mrs. M's surgeon and the SNF medical staff disagreed, so she stayed on for several months, incurring a bill of more than $20,000. When she challenged the HMO's decision through Medicare's appeal process, Mrs. M. won, and the HMO had to pay the bill for the extra time in skilled care.

A Medicare appeal of this type may take months to go through several levels of consideration, but it is important for patients to know that they do have this right.

9. The right not to be overcharged.
If you are in the fee-for-service program, Medicare limits your doctor to charging you 115 percent of a fee on a scale set by Medicare. Participants in an HMO may be charged some deductibles or copayments—for example, you may pay $10 for each office visit—but these charges are also regulated by Medicare. It is unclear, so far, exactly what limits, if any, will be placed on fees that you can be charged under some of the new Medicare programs, such as the "private fee-for-service" option described on page 114.

DECISIONS YOU NEED TO MAKE ABOUT MEDICARE

WHEN SHOULD I GO ON MEDICARE?
Unless you have dependable, better health insurance coverage through a current or previous employer, you should enroll in Medicare when you turn sixty-five. Waiting to sign up can cost you money, as well as compromise your health care.

As explained in the first section of this chapter, if you are not eligible for free Part A services and you delay signing up, you may have to pay a *one-time* penalty of an additional 10 percent of the cost of your premium. If you put off signing up for Part B, you'll be penalized 10 percent of the premium cost *for each year you delay*, with no limit on the number of increases. And these increases in the Part B premium remain in effect as long as you are on Medicare.

WHAT TYPE OF PLAN SHOULD I CHOOSE?

The types of plans offered by Medicare have been in transition for several years. If you choose a managed care or private fee-for-service plan, be aware that you are selecting an option that is relatively new to Medicare and therefore has a relatively short track record. If you are interested in joining Medicare managed care, learn as much as possible about all of the plans open to you before making a decision. One key reason for this is that each year a number of managed care plans have been withdrawing from Medicare, leaving patients to search for new plans and adjust to their new rules and providers. Three years after Medicare started offering the HMO option, thousands of clients had their care disrupted because their HMO withdrew from the program. While the managed care option remains available in most urban areas, in more rural parts of the country you may find that there is no managed care option at all.

Currently, says Joe Baker, associate director of the Medical Rights Center, "We do not yet have good information about the quality of health care" offered in a particular Medicare program. The 1997 Medicare law requires the HCFA to provide more complete information about each plan's costs, benefits, and services. But, says Baker, "I think we are about a decade away from having information on quality that is reliable and understandable to consumers." He suggests that for many people, the primary reason to join Medicare managed care is to have access to at least a partial prescription drug benefit. If the drug benefit is not important to you or is not offered, he suggests that traditional

Medicare may be better for you. Where does this leave you in choosing a Medicare option? "If I were advising my own grand-mother," Baker says, he would ask her to consider the following questions:

- Do you have the resources and time to manage your own care in the traditional fee-for-service program?
- Can you afford the deductibles and the coinsurance that Medicare requires, or a good Medigap policy to cover them?
- Can you afford insurance to pay for your own prescriptions?

If you answer yes to at least the first two of these questions, Baker suggests staying with traditional fee-for-service. Research suggests that people who are healthy tend to use Medicare HMOs, which may require less out-of-pocket expense and offer more benefits, such as physicals or some coverage for prescription drugs. But when people develop a health problem, they often return to a fee-for-service plan, apparently because they believe that they can get personalized attention for their specific ailment.

For many people, the key issue when choosing a health plan is the amount of control they exercise over their own health care decisions. In a Medicare fee-for-service program, you have more choice of doctors and other providers, and more to say about the type of treatment you will receive than in an HMO. Other factors to consider are:

- Cost: You'll generally spend less money out of pocket if you have an HMO than if you are in a fee-for-service plan.
- Location: Especially if you do not live in an urban area, you should choose health care providers that are geographically accessible.
- Prescription requirements: HMOs often provide much more prescription coverage than you would receive under fee-for-service care—but the amount may differ depending on which HMO you choose, and you may be responsible for copayments.
- Your lifestyle: If you travel away from home a lot, an HMO will cover your emergency care, but probably not other medical services you may want or need. If you're considering an

HMO, ask if it has a "point of service" option that allows you to use certain providers outside of the network.

• Tolerance for paperwork and bureaucracy: It's never easy or pleasant to complete paperwork for medical expenses, but you'll probably have less to do with an HMO than if you use fee-for-service.

• Reputation: Check with your state health insurance agency for information on any HMO you are considering joining, or any Medigap plan you are considering purchasing. Also, ask others in your community about experiences they may have had with particular plans or providers.

One of the most positive things about changes in Medicare, however, is that there are new tools to help you get the information you need to make a choice. If you use the Internet or have access to a family member or friend who can help you, visit www.medicare.gov and search the information listed under "Managed Health Plan Compare." This tool allows you to enter your zip code to retrieve a list of all managed care programs in your area. Then you can compare those programs according to many criteria, including a detailed list of the benefits offered—for example, mammograms or partial coverage of prescription drugs—and their costs and quality criteria. Quality measures include the percentage of clients of the plan who said they receive care when they need it, who receive prompt referrals to specialists, etc. If you do not have access to this Internet tool, call the toll-free Medicare line at 1-800-633-4227 to request a list of the plans that are available in your area.

SHOULD I SIGN UP FOR MEDIGAP SUPPLEMENTAL INSURANCE AT THE SAME TIME I ENROLL IN MEDICARE?

In general, for six months from the time you turn sixty-five, you may take advantage of an "open enrollment" period for Medigap. In this period, you may not be turned down for a policy, although you could be denied coverage for a pre-existing health condition for up to six months. Once the open enrollment period ends, no insurer is required to sell you a Medigap policy. This means that if you have some health problems, you should definitely make your decision about Medigap within those six months. It also means that if you put off buying a policy and develop a health problem at a later age, you may have trouble getting a policy when you need the coverage.

Because an HMO provides more comprehensive and preventive care, people who choose this option for Medicare do not need Medigap coverage. You also probably do not need Medigap if you have some supplemental coverage through a retirement health insurance policy. People who choose fee-for-service as their Medicare option, however, should analyze their own situation to determine if Medigap would make sense for them.

WHAT FACTORS SHOULD I CONSIDER IN DECIDING WHETHER TO BUY MEDIGAP?

Consider this: If you did not have Medigap or other supplemental health insurance and had to spend five days in the hospital in 2001, you'd owe a deductible of $798 for the hospital stay. That expense alone may be more than a Medigap premium, depending on where you live and which policy you choose.

According to the Kaiser Family Foundation, a non-profit health policy organization, "Medicare covers less than half of the total health spending of the elderly. . . . Beneficiaries spend on average $2,605 out of pocket—21 percent of their average household income—for health services and premiums." So if you don't have other insurance to pay those bills, should you buy a Medigap policy?

"It's a money and sense decision," advises Geraldine Dallek, director of health policy and author of the study on Medigap costs for the Families USA Foundation. "You need to figure out what your risk is," and whether you can afford to buy the extra coverage. Some states allow premiums to be based on your age—and to rise as you get older. Others may cost the same amount for people of all ages. To get detailed information on the Medigap policies available to you, use the "Medigap Compare" tool at the Medicare website, www.medicare.gov.

You may also contact the state insurance department in your state capital. You may find a list of these offices in the "Medicare and You" Guide and the "Guide to Health Insurance for People with Medicare" (see "For More Information" at the end of this chapter), or by calling the toll-free Medicare information number. The Medicare Rights Center suggests that when you get the information about Medigap options, you choose an insurance company that has an "A" rating in your state.

THE TAX FACTOR

As long as you continue to work—even if you are collecting Social Security—you must pay the 15.3 percent payroll tax, 2.9 percent of which goes to Medicare. (If you have an employer, the employer and you each pay half.)

The Internal Revenue Service treats the money you pay for deductibles, premiums, copayments, and other medical expenses you incur while on Medicare the same way it treats all medical deductions: if the total exceeds 7.5 percent in a given year, you may deduct the amount over 7.5 percent from your income. (See Chapter Seven for a discussion of the tax treatment of your non-Medicare health care costs.)

Because health care, and health care costs, become increasingly important as you grow older, Medicare potentially has an enormous impact on your retirement.

The comfort and pleasures of your retirement depend to a large degree on your health. And the health of your retirement budget depends to a large degree on how much money you spend on insurance and medical bills. The availability of Medicare over more than 35 years has contributed to both the improved health status and the longevity of countless Americans. Yet, as with any government program, the benefit you receive from Medicare depends in large part on decisions that you make personally—some times well before your retirement.

*   *   *

The time to inform yourself about Medicare's benefits and requirements is now, so that you can make financial decisions ahead of time that will enhance your retirement years. The three most important points that you need to keep in mind about Medicare are:

• Most people cannot start receiving Medicare until age sixty-five, even though you can go on Social Security at age sixty-two;

• Medicare is not free. In addition to the Medicare payroll tax you pay as long as you are working, you should plan to pay fairly significant medical expenses out of pocket even when you are in the program; and

• Medicare offers you a spectrum of options for the type of health care you want to receive. To get the benefits you want from it, you must participate actively in choosing your providers and challenge your doctors or your HMO if you think they are breaking the rules Uncle Sam requires them to follow.

FOR MORE INFORMATION

BY TELEPHONE

AARP
Call 1-800-424-3410 to request free copies of current publications that inform you about Medicare costs, benefits, and rights.

Medicare Rights Center (MRC)
For an extensive list of consumer publications on Medicare, or if you are having trouble appealing a denial of service or a bill with a Health Maintenance Organization (HMO) Medicare, call the MRC, 212-869-3850. MRC operates a hotline to assist New York State residents with Medicare problems and will try to help

callers from other states. Ask for a list of the Center's easy-to-read publications, including "Medicare Basics," "Medicare HMOs," and "Medicare Changes, Medicare Choices."

National Committee to Preserve Social Security and Medicare (NCPSSM)
Order these free brochures, available in English or Spanish: "Buying Your Medigap Policy," which includes a chart to help you compare policies offered by different insurance companies; and "Qualified Medicare Beneficiary Program," which describes how low-income Medicare beneficiaries may get help in paying their medical expenses. Contact NCPSSM at 1-800-966-1935.

Social Security Administration (SSA)
The SSA can answer questions about Medicare enrollment, entitlement, and premiums, and help you replace a lost Medicare card. Call 1-800-772-1213 (TDD 1-800-325-0778). For an overview of the Medicare program, request a free copy of "Medicare," (SSA Pub. No. 05-10043). The "2000 Guide to Health Insurance for People with Medicare" describes what Medicare covers, gaps in coverage, and summaries of the ten basic Medigap insurance packages. It also tells you how to find your state insurance departments and agency on aging, both of which can help you with questions about how state laws affect your Medicare and other insurance coverage. Your local SSA office has the forms you need to apply for Medicare Part A and B benefits. Call SSA's 800 number and press "5," then enter your zip code for the location of the nearest SSA office.

United Seniors Health Cooperative (USHC)
The 1998 edition of "Managing Your Health Care Finances: A Dollar and Sense Guide for Medicare Beneficiaries," which sells for $19, is a useful consumer handbook that offers guidelines for choosing a policy, a system for keeping track of medical bills, and sample appeal letters. To purchase it with a credit card or request a list of publications, call USHC at 1-800-637-2604.

**U.S. Department of Health and Human Services (USDHHS)
Administration on Aging (AoA)**
To contact local agencies that can help you obtain services such as health insurance counseling, call the Eldercare Locator at 1-800-677-1116. Give the name of your city and county, and a brief description of your problem.

USDHHS Health Care Financing Administration (HCFA)
This federal agency administers Medicare. For general information on Medicare, or to file complaints about Medigap policies, call the Medicare Hotline at 1-800-633-4227. You can also order the two HCFA publications mentioned above under SSA, plus other HCFA titles on Medicare, many of which list health insurance counseling toll-free phone numbers for each state. To report fraud, waste, or abuse, call the Medicare Fraud Hotline at 1-800-447-9477. (TTY: 1-800-377-4950)

BY MAIL

Medicare Rights Center
To request a list of publications, write to the Center at 1460 Broadway, 11th Floor, New York, NY 10036-7393.

ON THE INTERNET

www.ageinfo.org/elderloc
A public service of AoA, the Eldercare Locator Database can guide you to community groups that provide services to the elderly. Click on "Zip Code Search Form" to see contact information for your state's agency on aging.

www.medicare.gov
This site provides the most up-to-date information on Medicare costs and policies, as well as information on state and local contacts who can help you with Medicare problems. At the home page, choose "Publications" to read or download HCFA book-

lets such as the above-mentioned "2000 Guide to Health Insurance for People with Medicare" or "Medicare Managed Care." Click on "Medicare Compare" to find a comparison of the costs and services of Medicare HMOs located where you live.

www.medicarerights.org
At the MRC's website view their publications, member newsletter, and the latest information on Medicare.

www.ssa.gov
For Medicare information and publications, click on "Benefit Publications" on the home page.

CHAPTER SIX

Medicaid and Long-Term Care

Alice and Tom, a married couple, are both in their seventies and living at home. Tom has been diagnosed with Alzheimer's, and Alice, who also has some health problems, is finding it increasingly difficult to care for him. This couple has spent most of their savings on his medical bills, but don't want to move Tom to a nursing home because they're afraid that Medicaid would take the house and leave Alice with no place to live. Alice finally went to talk to a lawyer who specializes in these matters. He explained that if Tom went into a nursing home, Alice would be able to continue living in the house, continue to use their car, and in fact could receive a monthly income that would meet her needs, even if Tom was having his nursing home bills paid for by Medicaid.

Nationally, the average cost of nursing home care is $56,000 a year. This expense can rapidly consume the savings of an individual or a couple. Medicaid pays for nursing home care for older people. But in order to get the coverage, many people must first use up most of their savings to pay for the care privately. One way to avoid this is to transfer some assets to heirs, such as children, before you need the nursing home care. But you must follow complex, strict rules to accomplish this without breaking the law.

How can you protect your assets for your family, how can you be sure that a nursing home will provide good care, and what other government policies—such as tax breaks for buying long-term-care insurance—should you know about before making decisions about nursing home care? These are some of the questions that will be answered in this chapter.

WHAT YOU NEED TO KNOW ABOUT LONG-TERM HEALTH CARE

It is natural to be concerned about who will take care of you if you become frail or sick when you grow older. To plan for yourself and/or your spouse, or to figure out the best option for an elderly parent, you should get advice from medical and social services experts as well as from family. But you also should know about several federal government policies and programs that could determine what type of care is available and makes the most financial sense for you and your family.

Covered in this section is information on:

• Medicare home health care;

• Medicaid nursing home care, including the eligibility rules based on income and assets, and federal standards for care; and

• Tax deductions for receiving benefits from and paying premiums for long-term-care insurance.

HOME HEALTH CARE

Many people, even if they are frail or sick, prefer to remain in their own home if at all possible. People who are sixty-five and are eligible have a right to 100 percent Medicare coverage for an unlimited number of visits by intermittent or part-time skilled nurses and/or home health aides, medical social workers, and therapists, including physical and speech therapists. Medicaid, a program that serves people whose income is less than 75 percent of the federal poverty level, also provides home health care. State requirements and benefits may vary.

To qualify for Medicare home health care, you must meet these requirements:

• You need "intermittent" skilled nursing care or therapy, usually defined as less than eight hours of care per day or twenty-eight hours per week;

• You are confined to your home;

The Medicare Myth

Medicare provides for all the health needs of people sixty-five and over, including nursing care. True or false?

The answer is false.

It's appealing to assume that one all-encompassing program will pay for any medical expense, from flu shots to a hip replacement to residence in a nursing home. Unfortunately, no such program exists.

Not only does Medicare *not* cover some routine medical needs, as outlined in the previous chapter, *but Medicare also does not pay for long-term care in a nursing home.*

The only way Medicare actually will pay for nursing home care is if you have been discharged from a hospital, say, following a hip replacement operation, and require "skilled nursing" or "skilled rehabilitation" services. You must have been in the hospital for three days in a row, not counting the day you leave the hospital, and must be admitted to a Medicare-approved Skilled Nursing Facility (SNF) within thirty days of leaving the hospital.

Medicare pays 100 percent of the costs of your care in an SNF for the first twenty days. After that, in 2001 you must pay $99 a day for the next eighty days. If you need to stay longer, you must pay the entire cost.

- Your doctor says that you need the care, and helps set up the plan for you; and
- The home health care agency providing the care is approved to receive Medicare funds.

To be considered "homebound" by Medicare, you don't have to be bedridden. You'll qualify for the benefit if, in order to leave home, you need the help of another person or a device such as a walker or a wheelchair.

Family Caregiving

As the cost of nursing home care has risen and the proportion of elderly in the population is increasing, federal policy is placing a greater emphasis on encouraging families to find ways to meet long-term care needs at home, rather than in a nursing home. In late 2000, the Congress passed and the President signed a bill creating a new Family Caregiver Support Program that will provide $125 million to state governments to develop resources and services to assist family members who are providing care in their own homes. Among the services that will be available are information, counseling, support, training, and respite care. To find out whether you and your family might be eligible for services provided with these funds, call the Eldercare Locator for a referral to the appropriate state government agency. The Eldercare Locator phone number is 1-800-667-1116.

The one exception to the 100 percent coverage is for "durable medical equipment." This means, for example, that if you need to buy or rent a wheelchair or hospital bed, Medicare will pay 80 percent of the cost, but you must pay the other 20 percent.

MEDICAID NURSING HOME CARE

More than half of all nursing home care in the United States is paid for by Medicaid. Even middle- and upper-middle-income families often cannot afford to pay for nursing home care for very long. So currently, for an estimated 1.8 million older people who could not afford to pay with their own money, Medicaid is the only option.

With the benefits of federally financed nursing home care also come some demanding requirements:

- For the individual, meeting income standards and, sometimes, having to "spend down" most assets in order to qualify; and
- For nursing homes, meeting federal standards for quality of care and protection of patients' rights.

In this section you'll find questions and answers on the key things you need to know about Medicaid nursing home care: who is eligible, how the rules on income and asset transfers work, what benefits are provided, and federal rules on quality standards and patients' rights.

WHO IS ELIGIBLE FOR MEDICAID NURSING HOME CARE?

When Uncle Sam created Medicaid, the idea was to provide health care for low-income people who could not afford to pay for it out of their regular income. Thus everyone who receives Medicaid benefits—whether they're babies or mothers or retirees—must meet some type of means test or financial requirement. Another principle of the Medicaid program is that it's not just a federal effort: federal law requires Medicaid to serve people who meet certain standards of income and to provide a minimum package of benefits. But if a state wants to offer more services or make more people eligible for Medicare—and pay the extra costs—it may do so.

The basic ways to qualify for Medicaid nursing home care are: by meeting your state's low-income standard, or by "spending down" or using up your assets until you do not have the money you would need to pay for care privately. If your income is above the level your state sets for coverage, but you cannot afford to pay the costs of nursing home care for any significant length of time, you have to organize your finances to meet several Medicaid requirements.

HOW DO YOU QUALIFY FOR MEDICAID NURSING HOME CARE IF YOUR INCOME IS ABOVE THE POVERTY LEVEL?

There are three basic requirements:

Have no more than about $2,000 in personal resources for an individual and about $3,000 for a married couple.
The amounts vary depending on where you live. Resources that are not counted within the resources limit include: your home, if you plan to move back into it; home furnishings and personal effects; a car; $1,500 in burial expenses; and property that could produce income that could be used to pay for your care. In 1999, state limits on assets ranged from a low of about $1,000 in Missouri to a high of $5,000 in Florida.

In the case of a married couple with one spouse in a nursing home, Medicaid permits retaining more assets. The amount you can keep depends on a formula, but it must be within the federally approved range of at least $16,824 and no more than $84,120 for 2000. These amounts are in addition to money needed to pay housing expenses (rent or a mortgage), taxes, utilities, and insurance. The spouse at home may also receive an income, set by the state, which ranged from $1,383 to $2,049 in 1999.

"Spend down" resources that exceed Medicaid's asset limits.
If a married couple's assets are higher than Medicaid allows, they must spend the amount over the limit on the care of the spouse in the nursing home *before* Medicaid will take over the payments.

Except for a monthly "personal needs allowance," pay virtually all of your income to the nursing home.
The monthly allowance residents were allowed to keep in 1998, according to the AARP, was between $30 and $45 in most states, but as high as $75 in Alaska and $74.10 in Arizona.

HOW CAN I MAKE SURE ALL OF MY FINANCIAL ASSETS ARE NOT SPENT ON NURSING HOME CARE?

Parents often want to leave their property, whether it may be real estate, cash, or other assets, to their children or other heirs, and they want to avoid exhausting these assets on nursing home expenses. To keep the lid on the amount that taxpayers pay for nursing homes, Medicaid rules limit when and how you may dispose of assets in order to qualify for nursing home care. *In effect, these rules require you to think about and plan your financial strategies years before you or someone in your family may even need nursing home care.*

If you want to go on Medicaid, you will have to tell your state officials about any assets you have disposed of in the last few years. People who have given away or sold assets within the last three years in order to qualify may have to delay receiving the Medicaid benefit. The length of the delay will be the number of months that the assets you disposed of could have paid for nursing care in your state. In other words, to preserve your eligibility for Medicaid coverage of nursing home care, you need to plan in advance and transfer your assets at least three years before you might need nursing home care. Another way to do this legally is to put your assets into an irrevocable trust, but you must do this *five* years before you apply for Medicaid.

One essential element of this planning process, says Walter Feldesman, a New York attorney who specializes in eldercare, is to draw up a "durable power of attorney" designating another person to make decisions about property transfers and about your health, if you should become incompetent to do so at some point.

IS IT TRUE THAT A PERSON COULD BE FINED OR GO TO JAIL FOR BREAKING THE MEDICAID RULES ON TRANSFER OF ASSETS?

In 1996 Congress passed what became known as the "Granny Goes to Jail" law, establishing criminal penalties, including prison sentences, for people who "knowingly and willfully" disposed of their assets in order to become eligible for Medicaid nursing home coverage. The penalties also applied to any other person, such as a relative or professional financial planner, who helped older people do this illegally.

Advocates for the elderly as well as financial planners and elder care lawyers claimed afterwards that the law was vague

and confusing, and the penalties too severe. Congress respond-
ed by removing the criminal penalties on the individual whose
assets are transferred. However, anyone, such as a lawyer or an
accountant, who receives a fee for counseling a client to give up
assets illegally in order to qualify for Medicaid may still be subject to up to one year in prison and/or up to $10,000 in fines.

CAN MEDICAID USE THE MONEY LEFT IN MY ESTATE TO PAY FOR NURSING HOME BILLS?

Generally, Medicaid has the right to make claims for payment of
your nursing home care on your or your spouse's estate, but only
after you both are deceased. (This can vary, however, depending
on the state's laws.) In any case, Medicaid may not go after the
money if it has been inherited by a child who is disabled or
under twenty-one years old. Remember that the estate of a person who received Medicaid benefits should not exceed more than
$2,000, because if it does, that person committed a fraud.

WHAT BENEFITS DOES MEDICAID NURSING HOME CARE COVER?

In general, nursing homes that participate in Medicaid must
provide services "to attain or maintain the highest practicable
physical, mental, and psychological well-being of each resident."

Specifically, the Health Care Financing Administration
(HCFA), which runs Medicaid on the federal level, requires
participating nursing homes to offer the following types of
benefits:

- Nursing, rehabilitation, and related services;
- Medically related social services;
- Drugs needed by patients;
- Dietary services, including meals that meet residents'
nutritional and special dietary needs;
- Professionally directed activities that respond to patients'
interests and contribute to their well-being;
- Dental services;

• For the mentally ill and mentally retarded, treatment and services not otherwise provided or arranged for by the state.

CAN A NURSING HOME CHARGE A MEDICAID PATIENT FOR SOME SERVICES OR BENEFITS?

Medicaid specifies which services patients must receive in a nursing home without charge and which services the facility may charge for. Services that residents may not be charged for include: nursing care, meals, medically related social services, activities, care of the room and bed, routine items of personal hygiene (including soap and toothbrushes), over-the-counter drugs, and laundry.

Items that the resident may have to pay for include: special care, such as privately hired nurses; a private room, unless it is required for medical reasons; a personal telephone, television, or radio; some cosmetics and grooming items; clothing and reading materials; and special social programs or entertainment.

WHAT STANDARDS OF QUALITY DOES THE FEDERAL GOVERNMENT REQUIRE NURSING HOMES TO MEET?

A book about nursing homes, published by the National Citizens' Coalition on Nursing Home Reform, offers this story—one with a happy ending—illustrating how a facility can meet the spirit of the federal nursing home standards. (This is a shortened version.)

Mr. Zentoff was a fireman who worked the evening shift for thirty-two years. He continued to live on the same schedule—sleeping from 1 A.M. to 9 A.M.—at home after he retired. At eighty years old, diabetes and Alzheimer's were taking a toll, and he went to live in a nursing home. The staff at the facility became concerned that he was "walking around at night," and gave him sleeping medication. When his daughter came to visit, she found him to be uncharacteristically "anxious and lethargic." As a result of conversations between family and staff about Mr. Zentoff's routines, he was taken off the sleeping medication, and was exempted from going to bed around 8 P.M., when other residents retired. Back on his old schedule, Mr. Zentoff regained his energy, began socializing with residents and staff, and made a habit of going on evening rounds with the nursing home's security staff.

(Reprinted with permission from "Nursing Homes: Getting Good Care There," published by the National Citizens' Coalition for Nursing Home Reform, 1996.)

A 1986 report by the Institute of Medicine on unsafe and unhealthy conditions in nursing homes fueled a campaign that resulted in the Nursing Home Reform Amendments of 1987, which set up standards that facilities must meet in order to receive Medicaid or Medicare funds from the federal government. The right to individualized care, and to participation of both the resident and his or her family in planning for the care, are important principles that underlie all of the specific standards.

The "quality of care" standards require nursing homes to provide care that will prevent residents' condition from deteriorating unless the deterioration is "unavoidable." To meet the standards in twelve areas of care—including vision and hearing, activities of daily living, and nutrition—facilities must have certain types of medical, nursing, and social work staff whose training and work schedules meet minimum standards required by HCFA.

The law also gives a nursing home resident certain legal rights with regard to decisions that affect his or her care, requires regular surveys to evaluate care in the facility, and sets up a system for enforcing the standards.

HOW ARE THE STANDARDS ENFORCED?

Nursing homes that receive federal money are supposed to be inspected at intervals of anywhere from nine to fifteen months by state officials who are under contract to the federal government. These inspectors are required to observe and report on how well the facility is meeting the federal standards, and to meet with some residents and their family members to discuss

Legal Rights of Nursing Home Residents

The National Citizens' Coalition for Nursing Home Reform (NCCNHR), an organization that serves as an advocate for residents of nursing homes and their families, summarizes these rights as follows:

Rights to Self-Determination: To choose a personal physician; to participate in planning for one's care and treatment, as well as in choosing activities, schedules, and care according to "interests, abilities and needs"; to voice grievances about life in the facility as well as about care and treatment; and to organize and participate in resident groups in the facility.

Abuse and Restraint Rights: To be free from physical or mental abuse, to be free of physical restraints used for the staff's convenience, and not be to drugged for non-medical reasons.

Rights to Information: To receive information on these topics: results of the latest inspection of the nursing home, plans for correcting deficiencies identified in the survey, plans to change their room or roommate, and written information on their rights, on services provided, and on their costs.

Rights to Visits: To be visited by a personal physician, by a representative of the ombudsman program or health department, by relatives, and by organizations or individuals providing health, social, legal, or other services.

Thirty-day Advance Notice of Transfer to Another Facility

Protection of Money and Other Personal Property

Protection Against Medicaid Discrimination: A nursing home must have identical policies and practices for all residents, regardless of how they pay for their care.

personal experiences and observations. A facility that does not meet federal requirements may be subject to penalties, including fines, and could be disqualified from the program.

The National Senior Citizens Law Center, a public interest law firm located in Washington D.C., and other advocates for nursing home patients have expressed concern that the government's monitoring and enforcement activities are too weak, and do not provide adequate assurance that residents will receive the quality of care required by the government. As a result, Congress has required HCFA, the agency that runs the Medicaid program, to evaluate the current system and determine whether the rules need to be changed.

HOW CAN A PROSPECTIVE PATIENT OR PATIENT'S FAMILY FIND OUT IF A NURSING HOME IS MEETING THE FEDERAL STANDARDS?

Uncle Sam requires every state to have a long-term-care ombudsman program that provides advocates to speak and act on behalf of nursing home residents. These ombudsmen can also help individuals or families of individuals who are considering nursing home care learn about and evaluate specific facilities in their area. According to HCFA, an ombudsman should be able to provide the following specific information about a nursing home:

- The results of the latest survey (as described above);
- The number of complaints that have not been resolved;
- The number and nature of complaints filed in the last year; and
- The results and conclusions of recent complaint investigations.

LONG-TERM-CARE INSURANCE

An alternative to having Medicaid pay for nursing home care or paying for it out of your own savings is purchasing long-term-care insurance. A wide variety of policies are available on the market, with different requirements for coverage and different benefits. Insurance generally is regulated by state governments

Long-Term-Care Ombudsman Program

Every state is required to have an ombudsman program to serve as an advocate for nursing home residents and provide public education about nursing home facilities. You can locate an ombudsman in your area by calling the Eldercare Locator, a national information and referral system funded by the federal government, at their toll-free number, 1-800-677-1116.

Long-term-care ombudsmen have the following specific responsibilities:

• Identify, investigate, and resolve complaints made by, or on behalf of, residents related to action, inaction, or decisions that may adversely affect the health, safety, welfare, or rights of residents;

• Inform residents and their representatives about how to obtain needed services;

• Represent the interests of residents before government agencies and promote policies and practices needed to improve the quality of care and life in long-term care facilities; and

• Educate both consumers and providers about residents' rights and good care practices.

and, historically, the federal government does not have standards for policies that may be sold. However, since 1997 the federal government has offered new tax breaks to people who receive benefits from or purchase a long-term-care policy and has therefore established guidelines for policies that qualify for the tax breaks. These are the tax provisions:

• If you buy a long-term-care policy, you may deduct part of the cost of the premium from your federal taxes if your total medical expenses add up to more than 7.5 percent of your

---

Deduction for Long-Term-Care Insurance Premium

Uncle Sam allows you to deduct part of the cost of buying long-term-care insurance as a medical expense, if your total medical expenses are 7.5 percent or more of your income. The maximum amount you may deduct each year depends on your age. This chart shows the deductions allowed from your 2001 taxes.

Age 40 or less:	$230
Age 41–50:	$430
Age 51–60:	$880
Age 61–70:	$2,290
Age 71 and above:	$2,860

---

income. The amount you can deduct for the premium is based on your age, as shown in the box above.

• If you need to go into a nursing home or use other benefits in your long-term-care policy, you may exclude the value of those benefits—up to $200 per day or $73,000 for the year—from your gross income.

• People who are self-employed may include the cost of long-term-care insurance in their deduction (60 percent of premium costs, in 2001) for medical expenses.

To get the tax break for benefits you receive under a long-term-care policy, the IRS requires that the payments be made to a "chronically ill" person. The primary definition for "chronically ill" is that the individual cannot perform two out of five "activities of daily living" for at least ninety days, or to have Alzheimer's or some cognitive impairment that prevents the person from caring for him- or herself. "Activities for daily living" or "ADLs," as they are often referred to, are "eating, toileting, transferring, bathing, dressing, and continence."

DECISIONS YOU NEED TO MAKE ABOUT LONG-TERM HEALTH CARE

I'M JUST SIXTY YEARS OLD AND AM HEALTHY, BUT THERE'S A HISTORY OF SERIOUS HEART DISEASE IN MY FAMILY. SHOULD I TURN OVER THE ASSETS I DON'T NEED TO MY CHILDREN NOW, SO THAT IF I NEED NURSING HOME CARE IN THE FUTURE, MEDICAID CANNOT REQUIRE ME TO SPEND ALL OF MY ASSETS ON THE NURSING HOME?

People who own quite a bit of property, investments, or cash may be tempted to do this to make sure that their children benefit from what they have saved. However, the average sixty-year-old in the U.S. still has a life expectancy of more than twenty years, during which you may need or want to use those resources for yourself for something other than nursing care.

To understand why you should not move too hastily to turn your savings and other assets over to your children, consider this hypothetical worst-case scenario. Janet is a sixty-five-year-old widow, and she's in good health. She still lives in the family home, and she has about $100,000 in cash savings. When a neighbor unexpectedly offers her $200,000 for the house, she accepts the offer, intending to give the money to her daughter and move into an apartment. This would create several potential financial problems:

• Her daughter will have to pay taxes on $190,000 she receives from her mother's house sale, because the IRS only allows you to receive tax-free gifts of $10,000 per year.

• If Janet decides to remarry, she and her new husband may want to live in the house, or they may need the proceeds of the sale for their own living expenses.

• If Janet contracts a severe illness—Alzheimer's, for example—she will have fewer financial resources available to pay for her care.

Careful consideration of other options—including estate planning—could help Janet avoid any of these pitfalls.

MY SEVENTY-YEAR-OLD MOTHER'S HEALTH IS FAILING. SHOULD I SUGGEST THAT SHE GIVE AWAY HER SAVINGS SO THAT SHE WON'T HAVE TO "SPEND DOWN" TO QUALIFY FOR MEDICAID NURSING HOME CARE?

To get an idea of how to approach a decision like this, let's use the example of a hypothetical seventy-year-old woman we'll call Barbara. A widow with two adult children, Barbara has diabetes and suffers from failing eyesight and other chronic problems related to the disease. With the help of an aide who comes daily to make sure she has nutritious meals, and to assist her with dressing and bathing, until now Barbara has been able to stay in her own home.

The money Barbara receives from Social Security and a survivor's benefit from her husband's former employer cover her basic living expenses. But she has $75,000 in a savings account, and she's been trying not to spend it so that she can leave it to her children. Barbara's condition is getting worse, and she's concerned that within a year she may need to move to a nursing home. Barbara tells her social worker that she wants to give the money in the savings account to her children before it's too late, so it won't be spent on nursing home care.

The social worker warns Barbara that if she gives the $75,000 to her children, she could end up being ineligible for Medicaid nursing home care when she actually needs it—and also have no private resources to pay for the care. That's because Medicaid will delay her eligibility for the number of months that the money she gave to her children could have paid for nursing home care.

Let's say that in Barbara's home state it costs an average of $3,000 per month or $36,000 per year to live in a nursing home. She gives away the $75,000 in January 2002, and enters a nursing home in July 2002. The $75,000 would have paid for two years and one month ($75,000 divided by $3,000 per month) of care. Consequently, Barbara would not be able to get coverage until two years and one month after applying for Medicaid. Alternatively, if Barbara gave away $30,000 of the money, she'd have $45,000 left. That would more than pay for the ten months of care needed before Medicaid kicks in.

There is no limit on the penalty period for transferring assets illegally. If Barbara gave $120,000 in assets to her children, she would have to wait forty months, or more than three years, to qualify for the Medicaid benefit.

As this example shows, whether you should give away assets depends to some degree on how large those assets are. In addition to transferring assets at least three years before you need Medicaid eligibility, there is another way to protect them from being used up to qualify for Medicaid. It involves transferring them to a special kind of trust at least sixty months before you apply. The rules on asset transfers are complicated and the decision you make will depend partly on the rules in your state, so be sure to consult a financial planner, lawyer, or other expert before taking any action. (For help finding an expert, see "For More Information" at the end of this chapter.)

MY MOTHER NEEDS TO ENTER A NURSING HOME, AND SHE INSISTS THAT SHE WANTS TO LIVE IN THE ONE THAT IS ONLY TEN MINUTES FROM MY HOME SO THAT I CAN VISIT OFTEN. BUT I'M NOT SURE THAT FACILITY IS THE BEST ONE IN OUR TOWN. WHAT SHOULD WE DO?
The services offered and quality of care can vary tremendously among nursing homes. Despite the federal standards, complaints about quality of care and other treatment, as well as fraud, continue to stream in to ombudsmen and government agencies. This true story of an incident that occurred in Florida illuminates why you need to carefully investigate any facility you are considering:

A relative questioned charges to Medicare of over $1,000 for an "anti-contracture" device for his parent, who lived in a nursing home. The ombudsman went to the facility, and found that "Dr. A" had visited the facility and ordered such brace devices for almost all of the ninety residents. The contraptions were stored in residents' closets; they didn't help any of the frail, sick people they were given to, and in many cases they caused pain and skin abrasions. The ombudsman reported her suspicion of massive Medicare fraud to the appropriate authorities . . . Dr. A was ultimately convicted of organized fraud . . .

(Long-Term-Care Ombudsman, Annual Report, Fiscal Year 1995, U.S. Administration on Aging)

Proximity to the resident's family is certainly an important criterion, but as the Florida case shows, you should choose a facility based on a combination of research, information, and impressions you get from making personal visits to the facility. Facilities whose patients are on Medicare or Medicaid must meet the federal standards discussed earlier in this chapter. Even if a facility is not receiving federal money, all states have laws requiring them to meet certain standards. You can get information about nursing homes in your community—and how they have rated on inspections—from a local long-term-care ombudsman (see page 147) or by visiting the Medicare website (www.medicare.gov) and clicking on "Nursing Home Compare." This tool allows you to compare the ratings of nursing homes in a particular area on issues ranging from safety and nutrition to quality of medical care. A summary of ombudsmen's investigations in 1995 found that the most common complaints about nursing homes were related to accidents; issues of dignity, respect, and staff attitudes toward patients; lack of nutritious or appetizing food; personal hygiene; and staff not answering call lights or other requests for assistance—all problems we would not want ourselves or our relatives to have to experience.

The results of these surveys should also be available at the nursing home, and if the staff is reluctant to show them to you, this should raise your suspicions about the quality of care in the facility.

Should You Transfer Your Assets to Qualify for Medicaid Nursing Home Care?

Patricia Nemore, former staff attorney for the National Senior Citizens Law Center in Washington, DC, suggests that for a healthy person doing long-term financial planning, the main factor in deciding whether to transfer your assets should be whether you have the resources to pay for nursing home care if you need it—not a desire to leave your assets to adult children. To figure this out, she suggests, you should answer the following questions:

• Can you afford long-term-care insurance to pay nursing home costs if you don't qualify for Medicaid? Will your budget cover the insurance premiums, as well as your other family expenses?

• Can you afford to pay for nursing care out of your own resources? To answer this question, she advises asking several nursing homes in your area to determine what the costs would be. Be sure to ask for *all* the costs—not just the basic room and board rate—including fees for items such as a phone, television, or special meals. Assume that costs will increase by one or two percent above the inflation rate each year, she suggests.

• If you have a spouse or other dependents, what assets will be available to your family if you die? For example, your spouse may only get a portion of the pension you receive as a couple. If you transfer your assets to qualify for Medicaid, your spouse could be left with inadequate resources.

SHOULD MY SPOUSE AND I BUY LONG-TERM-CARE
INSURANCE SO THAT IF ONE OF US HAS TO GO INTO A
NURSING HOME WE WILL NOT HAVE TO WORRY ABOUT
PAYING THE EXPENSES?

About 40 percent of women aged sixty-five and one-third of
men in the same age group will need to spend some time in a
nursing home in the future. Women live longer and are more
likely to live alone, so they have a greater risk of spending more
time in a nursing home than men do.

Since the new tax deductions for long-term-care benefits
and premiums became law in 1997, the insurance industry has
mobilized to market such policies more aggressively. Buyer
beware! The tax breaks alone probably are not the most important factors to consider in deciding whether to buy long-term-
care insurance. That's because the tax deduction you may
receive for the cost of a long-term-care premium is limited in
two ways: you can only take it if your other medical deductions
are 7.5 percent of your income or more, and there is an annual
dollar limit on the amount you can deduct, depending on your
age (see the box on page 148). In addition, not all long-term-
care policies on the market will meet Uncle Sam's criteria for
tax breaks. Unless you read the fine print, you could end up
buying a policy that doesn't qualify for the tax deduction.

Consumers Union, an advocacy organization, warned in its
comments to IRS on the tax deduction: "The long-term-care
insurance market is complicated and filled with pitfalls for consumers. The new tax incentives make this complicated market
even more complex. Consumers need all the help they can get."
The organization also said that the laws do not require insurance
companies to provide enough information for consumers to
make informed choices, and called on the government to "police
the marketing" of these policies.

Walter Feldesman, an elderlaw attorney, suggests that people who are considering transferring assets so that they will
qualify for Medicaid in the future, but are still in their sixties
and in good health, should consider buying long-term-care

insurance to cover them in the three years after the transfer, during which time they would not qualify for Medicaid.

In sum, your decision on whether to buy long-term-care insurance should be based on cost and benefit data about a specific policy you are considering, and on the amount of assets you have now and would need to use for long-term care—not primarily on the tax implications. To see if the numbers work for you, get advice from an expert financial advisor who has your interests at heart, not just from an insurance agent. Another good source of information is the Insurance Counseling and Assistance Program (ICA) in each state (see "For More Information" to find one in your area).

THE TAX FACTOR

Attorney Walter Feldesman points out a little-known nuance in the interpretation of the long-term-care tax deduction. If you receive home health care benefits from your insurance policy, you may claim a deduction not only for the nursing services, but also for personal services such as assistance with bathing or eating, if those services are provided by the skilled health care aide who also provides medical or quasi-medical services.

In addition to the long-term-care insurance tax deductions, you or your family may be able to benefit from these adjustments to your federal taxes: additional medical expense deductions, or the Child and Dependent Care Credit.

People who pay out of their own pocket for home health care or for medical care in a retirement home may take a medical deduction for these expenses. As in the case of all medical expenses, you may only deduct them if the total medical deduction exceeds 7.5 percent of your income. Items and services you may deduct include:

• Nursing services, including giving medication and other activities associated with the medical condition—but not personal services or household tasks;

• The portion of the fee you pay a retirement home such as a Continuous Care Retirement Community (see Chapter 8) that covers medical care—as long as this amount is itemized in your contract with the community; and

• Social Security, unemployment, Medicare, and state employment taxes you pay a worker who provides medical care.

If the primary reason a person is in a nursing or retirement home is medical, it may be possible to deduct the entire cost of living there. Another possible tax break comes in the form of the Child and Dependent Care Credit. You may be able to take the credit if you pay someone to care for your spouse or other dependent—for example, your brother or sister—in the home. To be eligible, you must be working or looking for work. The maximum amount of expenses you can use to figure the credit is $2,400 per year for one person or $4,800 for two. The total amount of your credit ranges from 30 percent of the expenses, if your adjusted gross income is $10,000 or less, to 20 percent if your income is $28,000 or more.

*   *   *

Because the costs are so high and because people are living longer than in the past, the federal government is playing an increasingly important role in paying for and determining both the benefits and the quality of long-term care.

A person whose retirement is a decade or more away does not need to memorize all of the rules and conditions that define the government role. But as you, your parents, or others in your family make plans, you should keep in mind some key facts about the federal role in caring for older people who are frail or sick.

• Home health care can be a desirable alternative to living in a nursing home or similar facility. The federal government has programs that help with the costs, even if you have not been hospitalized before needing the home care.

• Facilities that receive federal funds must meet quality standards, and you have a right to insist that the standards be enforced.

- Medicare, which is available to virtually everyone who is sixty-five or older, only pays for nursing home care that is required as a follow-up to hospitalization.

- Medicaid pays for the nursing home expenses of people who cannot afford to do so privately, but to qualify, an individual or married couple must give up most of their savings.

- The federal tax law offers deductions and credits for nursing care expenses as well as receiving benefits from or paying a portion of the premium for long-term-care insurance.

And, most important of all: to minimize the potential disruption and stress—both psychological and financial—of addressing long-term-care issues, you can turn to many excellent sources of information and assistance, some of which are listed in the "For More Information" section below.

FOR MORE INFORMATION

BY PHONE

American Association of Homes and Services for the Aging
Ask this association of not-for-profit homes and other services for a list of their consumer publications on long-term care. Call 1-800-508-9442 or, if you are in the Washington, DC, area, 301-490-0677.

Eldercare Locator
This public service of the federal Administration on Aging (AoA) can put you in touch with sources of information and assistance in your community on issues including home health care, nursing home care, and long-term-care insurance. Call 1-800-677-1116 between 9 A.M. and 8 P.M. EST.

Internal Revenue Service (IRS)
For a copy of Publication 502, "Medical and Dental Expenses," and Publication 503, "Child and Dependent Care Expenses," call the publications order line at 1-800-829-3676.

Family Caregiver Alliance

This organization serves as a resource for families who need assistance in caring for older adults. Call them at 415-434-3388 or check their website on page 160 for useful information.

Insurance Counseling and Assistance Programs (ICA)

Through the Eldercare Locator phone number listed above, you can be referred to a counselor who will help you answer questions about choosing health or long-term-care insurance and resolve problems with Medicare and Medicaid.

National Academy of Elder Law Attorneys, Inc.

This organization publishes brochures with information on long-term-care issues. You can order "Long-Term-Care Insurance" and "Planning for Medical Decision Making'" for $2.25 each by calling 520-881-4005.

National Alliance for Caregiving

This organization provides resources and information on providing long-term care outside of nursing homes. You can call them at 301-718-8444 or see page 160 for their website address.

National Citizens' Coalition for Nursing Home Reform (NCCNHR)

This organization serves as an advocate for consumers of long-term care, and as the national resource center for long-term-care ombudsmen. For an extensive list of publications you can order about the federal law and how residents and their families may deal with nursing home issues, call them at 202-332-2275 or fax 202-332-2949.

National Committee to Preserve Social Security and Medicare

"Passages: Planning for Long-Term Care," is a pamphlet that offers basic descriptions of adult day care, senior companion programs, and other types of care and services that are available in addition to nursing homes, and suggests questions you should ask if someone in your family needs care. You may order it free from their toll-free number, 1-800-966-1935.

United Seniors Health Cooperative
If you or your family face a decision about long-term care now or in the near future, it's probably worth paying the $19.50 to order "Long-Term Care Planning: A Dollar and Sense Guide," published by this consumer organization. It describes the gamut of long-term-care alternatives, alerts you to pros and cons, and shows you how to evaluate the financial impact of each. To order, call 1-800-637-2604.

U.S. Department of Health and Human Services, Health Care Financing Administration (HCFA)
"The Guide to Choosing a Nursing Home" outlines six steps toward choosing a nursing home and monitoring care once a person is in the home. It describes the rights of patients and contains state-by-state lists of long-term-care ombudsmen, agencies that inspect nursing homes in your state, and insurance counselors. You may order by calling 1-800-638-6833.

BY MAIL

National Academy of Elder Law Attorneys, Inc.
See description in the "By Phone" section above. To contact them by mail, write to: National Academy of Elder Law Attorneys, 1604 North Country Club Road, Tucson, AZ 85716.

National Citizens' Coalition for Nursing Home Reform (NCCNHR)
See description in the "By Phone" section above. To get a copy of the publications list by mail, write to them at: NCCNHR, 1424-16th St. N.W., Suite 202, Washington, DC 20036-2211.

ON THE INTERNET

http://pr.aoa.dhhs.gov/naic
The National Aging Information Center, located at this address, has many publications you can order about nursing home and other long-term-care issues.

www.aahsa.org
The website of the American Association of Homes and Services for the Aging offers you the option of reading informational brochures online or ordering them by e-mail.

www.caregiver.org
The site of the Family Caregiver Alliance contains a wealth of information, including useful fact sheets about resources for providing both in-home and nursing-home care for the elderly.

www.caregiving.org
The site of the National Alliance for Caregiving also provides extensive information on caregiving resources and federal policy developments.

www.hcfa.gov
Select "Publications" to read the government's "Guide to Choosing a Nursing Home" and "Medicare and Home Health Care." Click on "FAQ" for some information on Medicaid rules and nursing care.

www.unitedseniorshealth.org
Here you can see and order from a list of publications available from United Seniors Health Cooperative (see "By Phone" section above). From the home page, click on "publications" and then on "links" at the bottom of the page for an excellent list of Web resources on long-term care and related issues.

CHAPTER SEVEN

Beyond Medicare: Additional Health Care Options for Retirees

George served in the U.S. Army for three years in the 1950s. He was not in active combat, and he received an honorable discharge. For most of his career, George was self-employed as the owner of a picture-framing business. Year after year he looked for—and often changed—health insurance that he could buy as an individual, and he paid dearly for it. George is sixty-one and plans to retire next year, when he turns sixty-two. He's been worried that his retirement income from modest savings and Social Security will not cover the cost of health insurance until he turns sixty-five and can get on Medicare.

One day George was talking with his neighbor John, who is also a veteran. To George's surprise, John told him that although George did not serve in combat and does not have a disability, as a veteran he is eligible, now as well as after he retires, to receive health insurance benefits through the Veterans Administration.

When you think about retirement, it's natural to think about Medicare as your primary source of health care coverage. But, as we've discussed in earlier chapters, people who retire before age sixty-five do not qualify for Medicare, except in certain very rare cases.

This leaves a lot of people with a dilemma: how do they find affordable health care coverage if they retire before turning sixty-five years old? More than 13 percent of people age fifty-five to sixty-four—3 million individuals—do not have health insurance. If you are one of these, getting coverage if you retire before age sixty-five is a continuing problem. But even for those who *do* have health insurance, the problem is exacerbated by several facts of life:

- As you get older, your insurance premiums usually go up;
- The older you are, the more vulnerable you are to health problems; and
- Once you've retired, your income will probably be lower than it was when you were working.

This chapter will describe several ways that federal laws can help you get the health care you need if you retire before age sixty-five.

WHAT YOU NEED TO KNOW ABOUT HEALTH CARE OPTIONS

Life would be a lot simpler if we could count on getting health coverage from our jobs throughout our working years and Medicare as soon as we retire. But with the way our system works currently, access to high-quality, affordable health care ranks as one of the top issues for people planning for retirement.

Some employers—usually large companies, with hundreds or even thousands of employees—offer health insurance to their retirees either until Medicare kicks in or throughout their retirement. Millions of Americans, however, do not receive retirement health insurance as a result of their employment. According to a study by Mercer/Foster Higgins benefits consultants, the percentage of employers who offer health insurance coverage to retirees declined from 46 percent in 1993 to 35 percent in 1999.

Other, related trends are also negative: the cost of premiums is going up, and, increasingly, employers are putting financial caps on the amount they'll spend for retirees' health benefits.

CAN YOU COUNT ON RETIREE HEALTH BENEFITS FROM YOUR JOB?

Do you have a right to retiree health benefits from your employer? Basically, the answer is no.

Even if health care benefits are currently a part of the retirement package offered by your employer, don't automatically assume that those benefits will be there in the same form on the day you retire.

As you do your retirement planning, remember these two basic facts:

• There is no law that requires your employer to provide you with health benefits in your retirement (except for the short-term coverage described in the section below on COBRA); and

• There is no law that prevents your employer from cutting back or totally eliminating retiree health care benefits.

If you and your family are among the 125 million people whose health benefits are covered by the federal Employee Retirement Income Security Act (ERISA), Uncle Sam requires your employer to give you information about the company's retirement health plan and any changes that are made to it. The basic information is contained in a Summary Plan Document (SPD) which you should receive when you take the job, and in notices of any changes to the plan that you should receive within sixty days after the change is made. If you are in an ERISA plan and don't have a copy of the SPD describing your health benefits, be sure to ask for it and read it.

However, a U.S. Sixth Circuit Court of Appeals decision in early 1998 confirmed that even if the SPD says the company will pay for your health coverage when you retire, if the company reserves the right to reduce or end the benefits, it has the legal right to do so. The case decided by the court involved 50,000 retirees of General Motors who had been promised free health care coverage and were later told they would have to pay their own deductibles and copayments in order to keep the insurance. This decision, as well as the recent studies of retiree health insurance, underscores the need to be prepared for the possibility that you may not get your retirement health insurance through your employer, and that even if you do, you can expect the cost to go up in future years. If you work for a state or local government or a church or non-profit organization, your plan will be subject to state insurance laws, but not to ERISA.

For a helpful explanation of how you can keep track of the retiree health benefits offered by your employer, get a copy of "Can the Retiree Health Benefits Provided by Your Employer be Cut?", a "Pension and Welfare Brief" published by the U.S. Department of Labor. You may order a free copy from the Department's brochure phone line, 1-800-998-7542, or read it on the Pension and Welfare Benefits Administration Website. To see the text, go to www.dol.gov/dol/pwba. Click on "Publications" and then on the title listed above.

The decline in employer-sponsored health coverage leaves the pre-sixty-five retiree with the expensive option of buying health insurance as an individual, on the open market; joining an organization that may provide insurance at more favorable, group rates; or taking advantage of one of several other options that are made either possible or affordable by the federal government. This section outlines several of the options available as a result of federal law.

CONSOLIDATED OMNIBUS BUDGET RECONCILIATION ACT (COBRA)

If you plan to retire before you turn sixty-five, this law provides a bridge to continuing your current insurance coverage for eighteen months after leaving your job. The great benefit of COBRA is that it entitles you to the same health insurance coverage and premiums offered to current employees of your firm at a time when it may be difficult to find a comparable alternative. But there is a downside: In addition to paying your own share of the premium, you must also pay the amount that was previously paid by your employer. The law does put a cap on the premium you may be charged—102 percent of the total cost that is paid for the same insurance by and for your colleagues at work.

You are generally eligible for COBRA benefits if your employer had twenty or more employees in the previous year and is a private company or state or local government. (People who work for the federal government or some church-related organizations do not qualify.) COBRA coverage is triggered by what the government calls "qualifying events." These are:

For Employees

Voluntary or involuntary termination of your employment for reasons other than "gross misconduct," or a reduction in your hours of employment below those needed to qualify for your company's health insurance plan.

For an Employee's Spouse

Termination of employment for any reason other than "gross misconduct"; a reduction in hours worked by the employee; entitlement of the employee to Medicare; divorce or legal separation; or death of the covered employee.

An employee who becomes eligible for COBRA may receive the continuing coverage for eighteen months. The spouse of an employee, however, may be covered for up to thirty-six months.

There are no federal rules governing exactly what type of benefits you can receive under COBRA (except that they be the same as offered to active employees) or your eligibility for them. But employers who offer group health plans must comply with requirements for reporting and disclosure, proper management of the plan, and enforcement of the rules under the Employee Retirement Income Security Act (ERISA), just as they must for their pension plans.

YOUR RIGHTS UNDER COBRA

Federal law requires your employer to provide you with detailed information about how this program works. Here is a list of your basic rights:

- To receive a Summary Plan Description (SPD) that explains your group health coverage within 90 days of joining a plan or receiving benefits from it, or within 120 days after the plan is subject to the reporting and disclosure requirements of federal law.

- To have a sixty-day "election period" in which to decide whether you want to continue with your employer's health insurance. The period begins on the date you lose your coverage or the date on which you receive a notice that you may choose COBRA coverage, whichever is later.

• To receive the same health benefits under COBRA as you did immediately before you left your employment (although in some cases, if you do not want to pay for "non-core benefits" such as dental and vision services, you may not be required to do so).

• To receive at least eighteen months of continuing coverage, unless you don't pay the premiums, your employer stops offering a group health plan, you enroll in another employer health plan that does not place pre-existing condition limits on you, or you become eligible for Medicare.

• To appeal a denial of a claim for benefits, according to rules that are explained in the SPD for your plan.

• To bring a lawsuit against an employer who does not provide employees with the required notices and election period.

Some additional, special COBRA rules apply to people who are disabled. For a detailed explanation of how COBRA works, read "Health Benefits Under the Consolidated Omnibus Budget Reconciliation Act," available free from the Labor Department's publications line, 1-800-998-7542, or on the Internet at www.dol.gov/dol/pwba. (Click on "Publications.")

MEDICAL BENEFITS FOR VETERANS

If you're a veteran, you may qualify to receive health care free or at reduced cost, even if you were not in active combat and are not disabled. The benefits are quite comprehensive. They include hospitalization, outpatient services such as rehabilitation and emergency care, and home health care (provided on a fee basis).

The Veterans Administration (VA) will decide if you are eligible based on your service record and your financial status. When the VA assesses your financial eligibility, it considers all of your income, including wages, Social Security and other pensions, and financial assets such as stocks, bonds, and bank accounts, and subtracts the amount of your debts to arrive at your income and net worth. However, the VA does not include the value of your home and your personal property as part of your net worth when it figures your eligibility. Here's what you need to know about the VA program:

Eligibility

Veterans will fall into one of seven "Priority Groups." Priority Group 1, veterans with service-connected conditions rated as a 50 percent or more disability, will be the first to receive services. The next several priority levels apply to veterans with varying degrees of disabilities, those who were prisoners of war, who are housebound, or who have a low income. The lowest priority, Priority Group 7, consists of veterans whose net worth is above the financial standard, and who agree to pay copayments for the services they receive.

Annual Enrollment

You can enroll in the VA medical program by filling out VA Form 10-10E, which is available by visiting, calling, or writing any VA location or veterans' benefits office. Once you've signed up, most veterans will be automatically re-enrolled each year. However, if Congress does not approve adequate funding, it is possible that some veterans with lower priority will not be able to receive services in a particular year.

Financial Standards

To receive VA care without cost, however, you'll need to meet the financial criteria. In 1998, these were:

If you are single: Your household income is $23,688 or less and your income plus net worth (not including your home and personal property) is no more than $50,000.

If you are married: Your combined household income is $28,429 or less and your income plus net worth is no more than $50,000.

If the VA has resources available and your income and net worth exceed the limits described above, you may still qualify for care if you pay some of the cost. The costs you have to pay are:

For hospital care: A copayment equal to the Medicare deductible ($792 in 2001) for the first ninety days of hospital care in a one-year period, plus an additional $10 per day fee. For each additional ninety-day period in the hospital, you'll need to pay half of the Medicare deductible plus the additional $10 per day fee.

Nursing home care: The full Medicare deductible plus $5 per day.

Outpatient visits: You pay 20 percent of the current charge to third-party health insurance carriers.

For prescriptions: You pay a copayment of $2 for each thirty-day or less supply of medication.

If you are the spouse or dependent of a veteran with a permanent and total service-connected disability, the spouse or child of a person who died in the line of duty within thirty days of active military service, or the survivor of a veteran with a service-connected disability, you may qualify to have some of your costs for medical care paid for under CHAMPVA, the VA Civilian Health and Medical Program. You can get information about this program by calling a toll-free information line, 1-800-733-8387, between 7:30 A.M. and 11:30 A.M. MT.

To find out if you qualify for VA medical care, look under the "Government" listing in your phone book for the nearest local VA facility. Call and ask for the "patient representative," who will explain what records you need and how to apply for benefits.

HMOS AND BEYOND: THE FEDERAL GOVERNMENT AND MANAGED CARE

Chances are that if you do not get medical benefits through some form of managed care now, you will in the future. The health insurance choices under the Medicare program include several types of managed care, including Health Maintenance Organizations and Preferred Provider Organizations. And if you retire before you turn sixty-five, you are likely to find that the most affordable health care option available to you as an individual is some type of managed care.

Does the federal government offer consumers of managed care any protections or rights?

Historically, insurance programs, including HMOs, are regulated by state governments, and states do have their own requirements for managed care organizations. But in recent years this situation has begun to change. As discussed in Chapter 5, Uncle Sam requires health care plans that participate in Medicare to guarantee certain rights—including the right to appeal denial of services and the right to information about benefits and services—to Medicare patients. If your HMO receives money from Medicare or Medicaid, it is likely that the rights and quality controls in place for those programs apply to your care, even if you are not on Medicare or Medicaid.

In addition, widespread concern about consumer rights in these federal programs has prompted a national movement to establish consumer protections and federal quality standards for all managed care programs. The 106th Congress, which was in session in 1999 and 2000, devoted considerable time and energy to considering broad patients'-rights legislation, but none was enacted. However, in the last days of the Clinton administration, the Department of Health and Human Services issued new regulations that require HMOs, doctors, hospitals, and other health care providers to adhere to strict rules of confidentiality of patients' medical records. If you'd like to know more about these rules, you can read a summary on the Internet by visiting www.hhs.gov and searching for the January 20, 2000, press release on this topic. In any case, when you consider joining a managed care program, you should always request information about the rights you would have as a patient and the quality standards that the program is required to meet.

MEDICAID

In addition to the nursing care benefits described in Chapter Six, Medicaid makes medical care available to some low-income older people. Generally, you can get Medicaid services if you qualify for the federal Supplemental Security Income program or have an income of 75 percent of the federal poverty level and assets of less than $2,000.

Medicaid also makes health care available to some older people who cannot afford to pay Medicare premiums, deductibles, and/or copayments under one of three programs: the Qualified Medicare Beneficiary (QMB) program, the Specified Low-Income Beneficiary (SLMB) program, or the Qualifying Individual (QI) program. For details on how this works, contact your local Social Security office or the office that administers Medicaid benefits for more information. (The name of this office varies depending on your state. It may be the Medicaid Office, for example, or Social Services. You can get the name and phone number of the appropriate office by calling the Medicare information line, 1-800-633-4227.)

MEDICAL SAVINGS ACCOUNTS (MSA)

Jim is fifty-four and he does not have any health problems. As a self-employed consultant, he pays $3,000 a year for his health insurance premium, but he rarely uses any benefits from the insurance. Jim wants to retire when he's sixty, and he knows that health insurance premiums inevitably increase as you get older, so he's been looking for an alternative to his current policy.

Recently a friend told Jim about a new type of health insurance called an MSA. He looked into it and figured out that by signing up for an MSA, he could both lower his health insurance premium and get a larger tax deduction. What's more, if he didn't use all of the money he spent for an MSA, Jim could actually earn interest or dividends on some of that money.

An MSA has two components: a high-deductible insurance policy to rely on in case of a major medical problem, and a savings account which, like an IRA, allows you to stash away money in a tax-deferred investment account. If you do not need the money for medical care, when you turn sixty-five and are eligible for Medicare, you may take the money out without penalty; or you can use it in place of a supplemental Medicare policy. MSAs are not for everyone. But for someone in Jim's situation, and for certain other people, an MSA may be the solution to the problem of health insurance in your pre-age-sixty-five retirement years. To locate companies that sell these policies, contact the Council at www.cahi.org or write them at 112 South West St., Alexandria, VA 22314.

MEDICAL SAVINGS ACCOUNT BASICS

To qualify for an MSA, you must meet narrow eligibility requirements. Also, Congress has limited the number of policies that can be sold because of concern that the tax breaks would take too much money out of the federal treasury. However, at publication time, the limit for MSA sales was nowhere near being reached, and the insurance industry was lobbying to remove the limit on the number of policies that could be sold.

Here are the basic facts about MSAs:

Eligibility
An individual or a family who is employed by a small business or are self-employed.

High-deductible Insurance Policy
An individual must purchase a policy with an annual deductible that is between $1,600 and $2,400 in 2001. The deductible for a family must range between $3,200 and $4,800.

MSA Savings Contributions
Each year individuals may deposit up to 65 percent of the amount of the policy's deductible in the MSA. Couples or families may deposit up to 75 percent of the deductible per year.

MSA Withdrawals
You may use the money saved and earned in your MSA for medical expenses without penalty until you turn sixty-five. If you withdraw the money and use it for any other purpose before age sixty-five, you must pay a penalty of 15 percent in addition to the income tax due on the withdrawal.

DECISIONS YOU NEED TO MAKE ABOUT HEALTH-CARE OPTIONS

WHEN SHOULD I RETIRE?

This may seem like an overly broad question to ask in the context of a discussion of health care options. But many people do ask this question. This is supported by the results of a 1993 poll, in which 61 percent of respondents said that if their employer did not offer some retiree health insurance, they would postpone retiring until they were eligible for Medicare. Today, the majority of Social Security recipients do retire before they are sixty-five. Because paying for all of your own health insurance and medical care can be so costly, you need to calculate the expense as accurately as possible when you are developing a budget based on your retirement income. If you do not have health insurance when you retire before age sixty-five, the cost of starting to pay for it at, say, age sixty or sixty-two may be prohibitive. People who have relied on insurance from their employer for most of their life may be shocked to learn that the premium they pay for coverage amounts to only about one-quarter or one-third of the total cost. That means that if you're paying $1,000 a year toward your health insurance premium while still working, you could end up paying $3,000 to $4,000 if you decide to use COBRA to fill the gap between retirement and becoming eligible for Medicare. Also, COBRA will only cover you for eighteen months. So if you retire at sixty-two, you'll still need to find coverage for another eighteen months.

If COBRA seems prohibitively expensive or you do not have access to COBRA, make a list of your other health insurance options. Include the federal programs and policies described in this chapter as well as sources of private insurance. Then research these options for private insurance by taking these steps:

• Find a local insurance agent or broker who can provide information about a variety of different plans;

- Ask colleagues, neighbors, and friends about their experiences with HMOs in your geographical area, and request detailed information on the benefits and services offered by those HMOs; and
- Identify professional or other organizations you might join to get health insurance at group rates.

IF I RETIRE BEFORE I AM ELIGIBLE FOR MEDICARE, HOW SHOULD I DECIDE WHAT TYPE OF COVERAGE TO GET?

When you have the information on several different types of health insurance, make a list or chart of all your options and their costs and benefits. On the list of pros and cons, be sure to include considerations such as whether you are committed to using the same doctors and other providers you use now, your health status, and where you can get the best care if you have chronic or serious problems. Don't forget that when you change health insurance plans you may be denied coverage of pre-existing conditions for some period of time after enrolling.

People who are in good health and are comfortable with a relatively low-cost, high-deductible (say $2,000) policy for a few years may decide they can afford to retire before qualifying for Medicare. But if you or your spouse has a serious health problem, the cost of both insurance and medical expenses in the pre-sixty-five years could be more than your early retirement budget can support.

In your budget calculations, don't forget to include the tax implications of the decision you make. (See "The Tax Factor" section on page 174.)

SHOULD I OPEN AN MSA?

Remember that right now the only people who may open an MSA are employees of a small business or self-employed individuals. The greatest advantage to an MSA is the tax savings. But to make an MSA work for you, you must be able to afford the cash outlay for the insurance premium, the tax-deferred savings account, and, before the MSA savings pile up, to pay any significant medical costs that may arise.

Let's say you are fifty years old, working for a small company that does not offer health insurance, and you plan to retire at sixty. Within a couple of years, you'll have enough money in the MSA to pay the entire deductible of your health insurance if you become sick. After that, the money will grow according to how you invested it. As long as you can afford to pay for both your health insurance policy and an annual MSA contribution, you'll get a tax break. When you turn sixty-five and go on Medicare, you can withdraw the contributions that have accumulated over fifteen years, without penalty, for any purpose. You will have to pay regular income tax on the amount you withdraw, however.

The scenario would be less rosy for a person with a tight budget and/or significant medical expenses. The high-deductible insurance premium is likely to be at least $120 per month or $1,440 per year; the older you are, the higher the premium will be. Add to that $1,040, in 2001, the maximum contribution to the MSA. And if you incur major medical expenses in the early years of your MSA, you may have to pay out of pocket to cover the deductible of $1,600 to $2,400, as well as any copayments required by your insurance policy. The less you put into the MSA each year, the less money you'll have to use toward the deductible if you need it.

THE TAX FACTOR

The federal tax code has numerous provisions that apply to expenses for health insurance and medical care.

MEDICAL EXPENSE DEDUCTIONS
If you spend more than 7.5 percent of your adjusted gross income on medical care in one year, you may deduct the excess from your federal taxes. IRS Publication 502 explains the types of expenses that qualify, including physicians' and hospital fees, medical and

hospital insurance premiums, and prescription drugs.

Even if you are on Medicare—and especially if your retirement income is limited—you may find that you will qualify to deduct medical expenses. Be sure to include the following on your list:

- Part B premium of $600 per year, for 2001;
- Part B deductible, $100 in 2001;
- Copayments—usually 20 percent—for expenses not fully covered by Part B. These would be for services such as visits to the doctor and lab tests;
- Medigap premium, which could range from $300 or $400 to more than $2,000 annually;
- If you are hospitalized, the Part A deductible, which is $792 in 2001;
- Prescription drugs;
- Copayments for hospital stays of more than sixty days, or stays of more than twenty days in a skilled nursing facility; and
- The amount you pay for the Part A Medicare premium—but only if you are among the few people who are not on Social Security and pay this expense out of pocket.

HEALTH INSURANCE DEDUCTION FOR THE SELF-EMPLOYED

If you are self-employed—for example, working as a consultant or operating a mail-order business or small retail shop after you retire—you may deduct part of the cost of your health insurance premiums. In 2001, the amount is 60 percent of the premium. See the chart on page 176 for rates in future years

INDIVIDUAL RETIREMENT ACCOUNTS

Normally you cannot withdraw funds from an Individual Retirement Account before age fifty-nine and a half without incurring a penalty. However, if you have medical expenses that are higher than 7.5 percent of your income, you may take money from a tax-deductible or Roth IRA (see Chapter Three) to pay the expenses without a penalty. You will, however, have to pay income tax on the amount withdrawn.

Health Insurance Deductions for the Self-Employed

These are the amounts that self-employed people may deduct from their federal tax in future years:

2001:	60%
2002:	70%
2003 and thereafter:	100%

MEDICAL SAVINGS ACCOUNTS

You may potentially benefit from the following tax breaks if you set up an MSA.

• If the premium for your high-deductible insurance, plus other medical expenses exceeds 7.5 percent, you may deduct it as a medical expense.

• If you are self-employed, you may deduct a portion of the cost of the premium for your high-deductible insurance policy, according to the chart and timetable above.

• You may exclude the money you put into an MSA each year (up to 65 percent of the deductible on your insurance if you're single; up to 75 percent of the deductible on a family policy) from your income for tax purposes.

• If you do not spend money from the MSA for non-medical expenses until you are sixty-five, you do not have to pay tax on the earnings.

• After you turn sixty-five, if you use the MSA money for a non-medical expense, you pay income tax on the withdrawal, but no penalty.

*   *   *

Maintaining your health and knowing that you have access to good health care can contribute significantly to your enjoyment of retirement, especially if you retire before you qualify for

Medicare at age sixty-five. But because our national health system is a complex patchwork of public and private services, achieving these goals can be a challenge. Uncle Sam offers some assistance in the form of both direct services and tax breaks that may make some costs of insurance and Medicare more affordable, but it is up to you and your family to figure out which federal programs or policies may benefit you. The key to your success will be in thinking ahead, starting to plan a few years before you retire, so that you can get a realistic idea of your options and take full advantage of them. As you do your planning, keep these key facts in mind:

• Learn about the benefits and costs of the retiree health insurance offered by your employer, and keep up with changes in the plan;

• Even if your employer offers an attractive retiree health insurance package now, there is no guarantee that the same benefits will be available to you at the time you are ready to retire;

• If you served in the military, whether you saw active combat or not, check into your eligibility for veterans' medical care benefits;

• Keep abreast and take advantage of federal requirements that you be informed about, and may challenge, decisions made by your HMO; and

• To the extent possible, calculate the potential tax impact of your options for health care.

FOR MORE INFORMATION

BY PHONE

Department of Veterans Affairs (VA)
"Federal Benefits for Veterans and Dependents" (Stock No. 051-000-00214-8), updated annually, contains basic information on veterans' health benefits and costs $5. You may order it using Visa or MasterCard by calling 1-202-512-1800. You may also call, request an order form, then fax your order and credit card

number to 1-202-512-2250. To talk to a VA staff person about health benefits, call the toll-free number, 1-800-827-1000.

Internal Revenue Service (IRS)

For details on how the medical expense deduction works, order IRS Publication 502, "Medical and Dental Expenses," and Publication 969, "Medical Savings Account," by calling the toll-free publications line, 1-800-829-3676 (TTY/TDD 1-800-829-4059).

U.S. Department of Labor (USDOL) Pension and Welfare Benefits Administration (PWBA)

For information on COBRA, request these two free pamphlets: "Health Benefits Under the Consolidated Omnibus Budget Reconciliation Act (COBRA)" and "Questions & Answers: Recent Changes in Health Care Law," by calling PWBA toll-free at 1-800-998-7542 (TDD 1-800-326-2577). If you expect to receive retiree health benefits from your employer, also ask for "Pension and Welfare Brief: Can the Retiree Health Benefits Provided By Your Employer Be Cut?"

U.S. Food and Drug Administration (FDA)

The FDA offers many free publications on health topics such as flu shots, buying medicine, and testing drugs in older people; and on women's health issues, including titles on mammograms and Pap smears. To request a list call the FDA office nearest you—listed in the blue pages of your telephone directory under "U.S. Government, Health and Human Services, Public Health Service," or call 1-888-463-6322.

BY MAIL

Council for Affordable Health Insurance (CAHI)

To receive four pages of questions and answers about Medical Savings Accounts, send a self-addressed, legal-size envelope with thirty-two cents postage to Council for Affordable Health

Insurance, Attention Anne Sewell, 112 South West Street, Suite 400, Alexandria, VA 22314.

FDA

For a catalog of free publications contact the FDA's Office of Consumer Affairs by writing to FDA, HFE-88, 5600 Fishers Lane, Rockville, MD 20857. You may then order a single copy each of up to twelve titles from the catalogue.

VA

The above-mentioned "Federal Benefits for Veterans and Dependents" may be purchased by mailing a check for $3.75, payable to the Superintendent of Documents, to Superintendent of Documents, P.O. Box 371954, Pittsburgh, PA 15250-7954. Include your daytime phone and the pamphlet's order number.

ON THE INTERNET

www.aarp.org
Search under keywords "managed care" for information about your rights and about how to choose an HMO.

www.cahi.org
The Council for Affordable Health Insurance's website has an explanation of how Medical Savings Accounts work and a list of vendors.

www.dol.gov/dol/pwba
On the home page of the Pension and Welfare Benefits Administration, click on "Publications." On the list you may click on and read the two publications on COBRA described in the U.S. Department of Labor listing under "By Phone."

www.healthfinder.gov
"HHS Healthfinder," a government-sponsored site, has links to numerous sources of information on consumer health and

human services information. Links include online publications, clearinghouses, databases, websites, support and self-help groups, government agencies, and nonprofit organizations.

www.irs.gov
At the home page of the IRS, choose "Forms & Pubs." Then select "Publications." Select a file format, click on "Publ. 502 Medical and Dental Expenses," and then choose whether to read the publication online or to download it.

www.va.gov
On the home page of the Veterans Administration website, click on "Health Benefits and Services" to read information on VA medical programs.

PART THREE

THE LONG ARM OF THE LAW

CHAPTER EIGHT

Your Retirement Home

John and Mary have lived in their "dream house" for forty-five years, and the mortgage is paid off. But now that they're retired and living on a fixed income, they're having trouble keeping up with maintenance and utility costs. Moving to a small apartment seemed unthinkable. Instead, they took out a reverse mortgage, which is a home equity loan that doesn't require any payments as long as you live there. With the extra $250 per month, they are getting along fine. They do not have to pay off the reverse mortgage until they sell the house, move away, or die.

WHAT YOU NEED TO KNOW ABOUT RETIREMENT LIVING OPTIONS

Where should you live when you retire? What federal programs may help you either stay in your own home or buy a new retirement home? What tax breaks do you get for selling your family home? Is it better to buy a home in a retirement community or to rent?

This chapter describes government policies you should know about before making a decision. One of the key things you'll learn is that federal tax policy could play a significant role in your decision about where to live. Because tax policies are so inextricably related to your housing options, this chapter combines a discussion of their impact in the section on "Decisions You Need to Make," rather than in a separate section on taxes.

For starters, though, this first section describes some basic federal policies and programs to consider in five different situations: if you want to continue living in your current home;

remodel your current home; purchase another house or apartment; live in a "Community Care Retirement Community (CCRC)"; or move to a rental property.

IF YOU WANT TO LIVE IN YOUR CURRENT HOME

Most of us have a deep attachment to our home, to the memories it evokes, and to our neighbors and friends. We've become fond of the shops and parks, movie theaters and restaurants, and community groups nearby that play an important role in our daily life. In fact, most Americans fifty years and older are so attached to their current home that even when retirement offers the opportunity to consider a change of venue and lifestyle, more than 80 percent say they prefer to continue living where they are.

Yet if you live on a fixed income in retirement, or on a lower income than during your working years, the cost of staying in your current home may be prohibitive. In the past, your only option may have been to sell your house and move to a home that is less expensive. However, recently many retirees have found they have another option. If you own your house, you can get a "reverse mortgage" that enables you to use the equity in your house to generate cash you can spend on immediate living expenses.

Here's how it works: if you're a homeowner who is sixty-two or older, you may qualify for a loan that is guaranteed by the equity in your home. Depending on the reverse mortgage and the lender you choose, you may collect the money from the loan in regular cash payments (for example, once a month), from a line of credit, or from a combination of both.

The prime advantages of a reverse mortgage are that you do not have to meet any income or asset requirements, and as long as you continue to live in the home, you do not have to pay off the loan balance. If you die and your heirs inherit the property, they will have to repay the loan, whether they do so with proceeds from selling the property or with other assets. As you draw money from your reverse mortgage, the loan balance will increase. But neither you nor your heirs will ever have to pay back any more than the present value of the property.

You can get a reverse mortgage that is insured by the Federal Housing Administration of the Department of Housing and Urban Development (HUD), based on limits that range from approximately $79,000 to $155,000 depending on where you live, through lenders all over the country. (You can find a list of these lenders at the HUD website, www.hud.gov/senior.html, by clicking on "reverse mortgages.") Fannie Mae, a home mortgage company chartered by the U.S. Congress, offers the "Home Keeper" reverse mortgage, which in 2001 may be based on equity in your home of up to $240,000. Some private lenders also offer reverse mortgages. Each type of reverse mortgage has its own rules, but in most cases the amount of the loan depends on your age, the value of your house, loan costs, and the limit on the amount of equity in your home that you may use to guarantee the loan.

For example, when this book was written, a person who was sixty-five could borrow up to 26 percent of the home's value, a seventy-five-year-old could borrow up to 39 percent, and an eighty-five-year-old could borrow up to 56 percent for a reverse mortgage secured through HUD. The cash you receive from the reverse mortgage will not lower or make you ineligible for your Social Security or Medicare eligibility or benefits. However, if you receive benefits from a federal program with an income qualification—such as Medicaid or Food Stamps—the increased income from the reverse mortgage could result in a cut or loss of eligibility.

The limits on the amount you can borrow, the types of property that are eligible, interest rates, the cost of fees required for the transaction, and the form in which you get the loan—for example, line of credit or monthly payment—depend on the type of reverse mortgage you get. Fees for loan origination (points) and other closing costs can usually be wrapped into the mortgage. If you want to get a reverse mortgage from HUD or Fannie Mae, you must participate in a consumer counseling session so that you can figure out the pros and cons of a reverse mortgage in relationship to your own finances.

Attractive as a reverse mortgage may sound, you should be aware of and research the following potential disadvantages thoroughly before making a decision:

• As for any loan, you must pay certain fees such as closing costs, insurance premiums, and mortgage servicing fees. These may be folded into the loan, however, so you do not have to pay them in cash; and

• Because you are not actually paying off the loan each month, and the interest is building up, your debt is growing. This means that, for example, if you take out a reverse mortgage at age sixty-five, if your heirs inherit your home when you pass away at age eighty-five, the value of the home may be substantially less than when you took out the mortgage.

Bronwyn Belling, a former reverse mortgage specialist for the AARP, warns that the costs of reverse mortgages require "substantial upfront fees," and that the costs of different reverse mortgages "can vary enormously." Before deciding on a reverse mortgage, she suggests, you should request the "total annual loan cost" (TALC), a standard federal measure that enables you to compare exact costs of different types of reverse mortgages. A nonprofit, consumer-oriented website, www.reverse.org tells you how to get and use the TALC. "Personal Reverse Mortgage Analysis," published by the National Center for Home Equity Conversion and described in the "For More Information" section at the end of this chapter, can also help you get a complete rundown of the costs of reverse mortgages you are considering. The site also contains alerts and cautions to help you steer clear of disreputable lenders and get the best terms if you decide to apply for a reverse mortgage.

IF YOU WANT TO REMODEL YOUR HOME

Ann and Tom are trying to decide if they should stay in their home or move. Since her recent hip operation, Ann, who is seventy, has been using a wheelchair when she goes out of the house. Getting around inside would be easier if she could use

---

Reverse Mortgage Alert

A few years ago, HUD announced that many retired home-owners had been charged fees—up to $10,000 or even more—for information they could have received about reverse mortgages for no charge from a HUD toll-free information line. As a result of the extensive publicity of this scam, HUD officials say the problem has pretty much disappeared. But if you need information or counseling about a reverse mortgage, be on your guard and do not pay for it. Instead, call HUD at 1-800-217-6970 to get the name of an approved housing counseling agency that offers free assistance, or send for a copy of a list of counselors who have pledged to meet ethical standards on issues including disclosure of consumer options and counselor interests, confidentiality, and reporting financial exploitation. You can get the list from AARP's National Center for Home Equity Conversion, which is listed in the "For More Information" section at the end of this chapter.

---

the chair, but some of the doorways are too narrow. Tom, who is seventy-two, has been complaining about the draft coming into the house from windows and doors that are not adequately sealed and about the ever-rising heating bills.

As you get older, living in an unsafe home can make you vulnerable to falls and other accidents that can jeopardize your ability to remain independent. This safety issue has become so prevalent that the federal government now operates a National Center for Injury Prevention and Control. The Center reports that falls are the leading cause of injury and deaths among people age sixty-five and older, and that 60 percent of fatal falls occur in the home. In the information section at the end of this chapter, you'll find resources, including checklists, that can help you figure out how to remodel your home so that you can continue to live there safely as you get older. Even what might appear to be minor remodeling changes can make the difference between living safely and economically in your current home and feeling compelled to move. If you want to install ramps, widen doorways, or make other capital improvements whose purpose is medical care for yourself or your spouse, you can deduct the cost of these from your income taxes as medical expenses. However, don't forget that the IRS only allows you to deduct medical expenses if they exceed 7.5 percent of your adjusted gross income. (See page 195 for more details.) If your goal is to be more comfortable and to reduce the bills by making your home more energy-efficient, look into refinancing with a mortgage insured by HUD under its Energy Efficient Mortgage Program. These mortgages allow you to wrap in the greater of 5 percent of the property's value or $8,000 to make the necessary improvements. To qualify for this financing, you'll need to hire an energy consultant to determine if this makes sense for your particular property. (You can also use this program to purchase a new home and add the cost of improvements in energy efficiency to the mortgage.)

Other options for paying for remodeling are the Fannie Mae Home Style Remodeler loan, for up to $50,000, or the Fannie Mae Home Style Energy loan, for up to $20,000.

IF YOU WANT TO BUY A NEW HOME

Is your retirement dream home a renovated farmhouse in the country? Or a condo that's walking distance from the beach? If so, the government may be able to assist you in three different ways:

- By insuring your mortgage for the new home;
- By providing access to a reverse mortgage; and
- By enforcing federal laws that prohibit age discrimination in the approval of mortgage financing.

FHA-Insured Loans

You may qualify for an FHA-insured mortgage to buy a single-family residence, including a condominium or a cooperative, or a farm or other rural property. Depending on the type of property you are buying, FHA-insured mortgages have different eligibility requirements and different loan limits. For more information on how to get the details, check the HUD references listed at the end of this chapter.

Reverse Mortgage for Home Purchase

You may also want to look into a special type of reverse mortgage offered by Fannie Mae—one that you can use not to stay in your current house but to buy a new one. Known as the "Home Keeper Home Purchase," this option may be most attractive if you're selling your current home and can afford a substantial down payment on a new one. The advantage is that, as in the case of the regular reverse mortgage, you do not have to pass any income or asset tests, and you don't have to repay the loan as long as you live in the new home.

The following example from Fannie Mae illustrates how this way of buying a home without having to worry about a monthly mortgage payment works: Mrs. Jones is seventy-six, and she's selling her home for $75,000. She wants to buy a new home for $115,000. To pay for the new home with cash, she'll need to take $40,000 out of her savings and add it to the proceeds of selling her current property. Instead, Mrs. Jones decides to get a Home Keeper Home Purchase loan of $60,000. She takes $55,000 from the sale of her home and adds it to the Home Keeper loan to buy the new home. This gives Mrs. Jones the following advantages: She has $20,000 in cash, she does not have to tap her savings to buy the new home, and she will not have any mortgage payments.

As with any other mortgage, Mrs. Jones will be charged some fees and closing costs. If she moves out of the new house, she'll have to repay the loan. And if the property goes to her heirs, they will be required to pay back the loan.

Credit Opportunity

Finally, federal law says that a mortgage company or bank may not deny you financing simply because of your age, and requires that income you will receive from Social Security or a pension be considered in determining your eligibility for the mortgage.

CONTINUING CARE RETIREMENT COMMUNITIES (CCRC)

People who want to live in an environment that offers access to a range of medical services as well as lodgings can opt for a "Continuing Care Retirement Community," or CCRC. According to the American Association of Homes and Services for the Aging (AAHSA), an organization of nonprofit organizations that provide housing and other services to the elderly, CCRCs provide "a continuum of housing, services, and health care, centrally planned, located, and administered." According to AAHSA, the housing offered at a CCRC may include the following options:

• "Independent living" units such as apartments, cottages, or single-family homes;

• "Assisted living" units that offer residents access to help with daily activities such as bathing and dressing; and

• "Nursing care," including short- or long-term care, including "rehabilitative and 'round the clock" nursing services.

CCRCs are privately owned, but Uncle Sam gets involved because when you move to one of these communities you sign a contract to pay for your residence and other fees—for example, for medical services, meals, or amenities such as access to transportation—that may have an impact on federal taxes. (See page 193 of this chapter on "Decisions You Need to Make" for a discussion of the relationship of CCRCs and federal taxes.)

Also, residents of a CCRC may use their Medicare and Medigap coverage to pay for their health care. See Chapter Six for a discussion of how federal policy may influence the availability and cost of living arrangements for retired people who require long-term nursing care.

LIVING IN A RENTAL APARTMENT OR HOUSE

HUD provides some incentives for developers to build housing that is designed for seniors with a low or moderate income. To learn about the availability and eligibility requirements of senior housing in your community, contact the closest HUD field office. In some communities you may also be able to get information from your Area Agency on Aging. (See the "For More Information" section at the end of this chapter.)

If you decide to live in a rented apartment or house during your retirement, you should know that federal law prohibits landlords from discriminating against people because of a disability or the perception that they have a disability. Except in the case of housing specifically designed for older people, "there is nothing in federal law that prohibits discriminating against someone in housing on the basis of age," explains Stephanie Edelstein, a lawyer on the staff of the American Bar Association's Commission on Legal Problems of the Elderly. Still, many older people have physical or mental impairments that do bring them under the protection of these laws. If a landlord asks you, for example, to have someone co-sign a lease with you to guarantee that you will pay the rent, the request could violate federal law if it is based on a "perception" of disability based on the fact that you are of a certain age. In addition, "if a landlord tells you that you must provide a phone number to call in the case of an emergency, or a letter from your doctor saying that you are in good health," Edelstein says, that could also be considered discrimination.

HUD suggests that some of the telltale signs that a landlord or real estate agent may be discriminating against a person who is frail or disabled include comments such as:

• "You can't live here because if you did my insurance rates would increase";

• "We have a no-pets rule," to a person who requires a seeing-eye dog; or

• "Your wheelchair will cause too much damage to the walls, and I am worried about my liability if there is a fire."

In fact, if you have a disability, the Fair Housing Act gives you the right to make "reasonable modifications" to make the home you rent safer or more comfortable. Such modifications may include installing a ramp to help you get a wheelchair through

Your Housing Rights

Federal law prohibits discrimination in housing on the basis of race or color, national origin, religion, sex, familial status, or handicap. This law applies to housing being sold or rented, and also prohibits mortgage lenders from refusing you a loan or imposing special conditions on a loan because of one of these factors. The law also gives renters the right to make "reasonable modifications," such as installing grab bars in the bathroom of your apartment or house to accommodate a disability.

If you believe your rights to housing have been violated, you should contact HUD to file a claim against the landlord, owner, mortgage company, or other individual or organization you believe has violated the law.

To get a copy of HUD's Discrimination Complaint Form 903, or to find the location of the nearest HUD office where you can file a charge, call their toll-free number: 1-800-669-9777. HUD may investigate the complaint, or—if your state or local housing law is similar to the federal law—refer it to a state or local agency. If HUD or another agency finds there is reasonable cause to believe discrimination has occurred, your options include trying to resolve the case by conciliation, using a government attorney to take your case to court, or hiring your own attorney to do so. HUD is supposed to complete its initial investigation within 120 days of your filing a claim, but pursuing a fair housing case can take many months, depending on the legal action required and the backlog in the jurisdiction where it is filed.

the front door, providing a parking space that is close to the door, or installing grab bars in the bathroom.

As you might expect, federal laws on these issues have a lot of complex fine print. What's important to remember is that if a landlord refuses to rent to you or to allow you to modify your apartment or house—and you believe the reason is because you are disabled or because the landlord or real estate agent perceives you as disabled—you should contact a local HUD office as soon as possible to discuss the possibility of filing a claim and having the charge investigated.

DECISIONS YOU NEED TO MAKE ABOUT YOUR RETIREMENT HOME (AND THE TAX IMPACTS OF THESE DECISIONS)

Betsy McCreary, who has lived in New York City for fifty years and worked in the publishing industry, decided to use her retirement to explore and enjoy all of the neighborhoods and activities she didn't have time for when she was working. She resides in the same rent-controlled, midtown Manhattan apartment where she has lived for thirty-four years.

In contrast, her brother John, who retired from a military career, moved to an old farmhouse in the Virginia countryside where he spent the first decade of his retirement creating and operating a vineyard and a winery. Now John's moved on to video production, but he still chooses to live in this rather isolated but beautiful spot.

Before you make a decision about where to live in retirement you need to consider many factors—the daily lifestyle you want; proximity of children, grandchildren, or other relatives and friends; the type of climate you enjoy; and your health or medical needs. Ideally you should consider these personal and lifestyle factors first. Then you need to face reality. What can you afford? As usual, when it comes to financial issues, Uncle Sam enters the picture. Because tax impact can be crucial when you're analyzing the pros and cons of where and how to live, this section combines the discussion of "Decisions You Need to Make" with information on the potential tax impact of your decisions.

SHOULD I CONTINUE TO LIVE IN MY CURRENT HOME AFTER RETIREMENT?

If your answer is yes, based on personal issues like those mentioned above, then you need to calculate whether your income will be sufficient to keep up the mortgage and/or expenses and taxes, and whether you need to remodel the home to make it safer or more comfortable.

Staying in your current home will probably be much more economical if the mortgage is already paid off. If you don't own the house free and clear, you'll need to figure out if your retirement income will be high enough for you to continue the payments. Regardless of whether you are retiring soon or a decade from now, don't forget that mortgage interest can provide a big deduction on your federal taxes. However, if you're close to paying off the house, most of your monthly payment is likely to be principal, which is not deductible. And even if you will not have to make mortgage payments, you'll need to make sure that your retirement income will cover the cost of utilities, repairs, insurance, and property taxes. State and local property taxes are deductible on your federal return, but you'll only really get the benefit if your total deductions exceed the standard deduction, which was $4,400 for a single individual and $7,350 for a married couple filing jointly in 2000. (If you're 65 or older, the respective rates are $5,000 and $8,200.)

People who take out a reverse mortgage in order to stay in their home will not benefit from the mortgage interest deduction until and unless they sell the property. If a property with a reverse mortgage has not appreciated enough to cover the interest on the loan, you may not get a tax break on it at all. However, you generally will not have to pay income tax on the money you receive from the reverse mortgage—whether it's in a lump sum, a monthly payment, or some other form of payment. The main exception to this is if you take the money in the form of annuity payments, which may be partially taxable.

SHOULD I STAY IN MY CURRENT HOME, BUT MAKE IT SAFER OR MORE ENERGY-EFFICIENT?

If you want to continue living in your home—as most people do—you should evaluate whether it meets your current and future physical needs. If it requires repairs or remodeling, do you want to undertake these projects, and can you afford the cost? If you or your spouse has a medical problem, you may be able to take some or all of the cost of some capital improvements to your home as a medical deduction on your federal form. However, to deduct any medical expenses at all, the annual total of those expenses must exceed 7.5 percent of your adjusted gross income. Also, if the improvements you make increase the value of the home, IRS will reduce your deduction by the amount of increase in the value in your property. IRS offers this example of how the medical deduction for capital expenses might work: Your doctor recommends that, because of a heart ailment, you install an elevator to go up the stairs. The elevator costs $2,000, and increases the value of your house by $1,400. You will be able to deduct only $600 as a medical expense.

Internal Revenue Service Publication 502 lists the following improvements to your home as acceptable medical deductions "if their main purpose is medical care for you, your spouse or a dependent" (for a complete list, order this publication by calling 1-800-429-3676):

- Constructing entrance or exit ramps;
- Widening doorways at entrances or exits, or inside the house;
- Modifying stairways;
- Installing railings, support bars, or other modifications to bathrooms; and
- Grading the ground to provide access to the house.

SHOULD I SELL THE HOME I OWN?

A few years ago, *The New York Times* reported that a doctor and his wife, who had bought an entire island for $1 million, were expecting to sell it soon for $1.75 million—and pay little or no capital gains tax. How could they qualify for such a windfall? The explanation is that, like many other people who are close to retiring or already retired, they're taking advantage of a tax law that allows a married couple to exempt up to $500,000 in profit on the sale of a primary residence.

For the doctor and others who made savvy real estate investments in their homes and have avoided selling because they didn't want to pay the capital gains, the Taxpayer Relief Act of 1997 brought significant relief indeed. If you're in this category, the law could mean extra cash in your pocket to use as you please—for example, to buy another retirement home or to travel—as well as increased freedom to think about selling the house without feeling constrained by a tax bite you can't afford.

Previous requirements that you had to be at least fifty-five years old to benefit from the capital gains exclusion and/or roll the gain into purchasing a new residence within two years of selling the old one are no longer in effect. Under the new law, when you sell your house, you may exclude the capital gains of up to $250,000 for an individual and $500,000 for a couple from your federal tax. To qualify for the exclusion, you must have owned and lived in the residence for at least two of the last five years prior to selling it. You may also sell a home and benefit from the exclusion as many times as you want, as long as you live in each residence you buy for at least two years before selling it. (However, if you lived in the house for less than two years due to a change in your health or your job, you may still qualify for a tax break. See IRS Publication 523 for details.)

For people who might want to stay in their home, but would also like to benefit from an increase in value and from the tax break, Washington, DC, real estate lawyer Benny Kass suggests this strategy: Sell your house to your child or children, but continue to live in it and pay the rent to your kids. You'll get some extra cash, because you can keep the profit up to the limits of the exclusion. Your children will receive the rental income—hopefully, enough to pay the mortgage and other expenses of maintaining the house—and, if the value of your estate will exceed more than $675,000 (this is in 2001; the figure will be $700,000 for 2002 and 2003) for each child, this will reduce or prevent your kids from having to pay inheritance taxes on the house in the future.

SHOULD I BUY A NEW HOME FOR MY RETIREMENT YEARS?

Let's say you and your spouse own and live in a four-bedroom house in the city, which has a market value of $300,000, compared to the $200,000 it cost when you bought it. You want to retire to a two-bedroom condo in the suburbs or in a beach community. With the $300,000 from selling the city house—free of capital gains tax—you can undoubtedly purchase a very nice two-bedroom condo and still have money left over. There will be no tax penalty for the downsizing. You'll have to figure out, however, whether it makes more sense to keep the proceeds of selling your house and get a mortgage, if you qualify for one, and benefit from the mortgage interest deduction, or to buy the new home outright. Because this type of calculation requires analysis of all sources of your retirement income and their tax consequences, ask your financial or tax advisor to help you figure this one out.

SHOULD I MOVE INTO A CCRC?

This choice is, first and foremost, a lifestyle decision: Do you want to live in a community where you will have easy access to various levels of medical and other services that you need now or may need in the future? If the answer is yes, and if you can afford a CCRC that appeals to you (a recent government study cited their cost as ranging from $34,000 for a studio apartment for one person to $439,600 for a two-bedroom home for a couple) and want to buy your CCRC home rather than rent it, be sure to consult an expert on the tax implications of both the home purchase and the fees you will have to pay for health and other services. The condo, co-op, or other home you buy in a CCRC carries with it the same obligations and risks as any other real estate purchase. When you move to a CCRC you may also purchase pre-paid health care coverage, and some of the cost of this fee may be deductible as a medical expense.

SHOULD I BE (OR BECOME) A RENTER IN MY RETIREMENT YEARS?

Renters reap few, if any, tax benefits from Uncle Sam—but they also don't have to worry about the expense and hassle of home maintenance, real estate taxes, and property insurance. If you're tired of doing all of this yourself, look for a building or a development with a superintendent and let someone else take care of it.

I'VE ALWAYS WANTED TO LIVE IN ANOTHER COUNTRY. WHAT FEDERAL POLICIES DO I NEED TO KNOW ABOUT BEFORE MAKING A DECISION?

Nicole Mewhinney of Winston-Salem, North Carolina, lived in France for twenty years. When she became eligible for Social Security, she had her benefits deposited in a bank account in the U.S. that she could draw on in France. She never had problems getting her Social Security or paying her taxes from overseas, but there was one problem that played a big role in her decision to return to live in America: not being eligible for Medicare.

Mewhinney is healthy, but after several years of paying for private health insurance, she says, she re-evaluated her situation. "I'm sixty-nine, and going to be seventy next July," she explained. "At some point you have to plan for the future."

Retirement should be a time when you can live out your fantasies and experiment with experiences that were not available in your working years. High on that list of experiences may be living in another country. Thousands of Americans have retired in Mexico, for example, which offers the advantage of having a common border and being close enough to keep in touch with relatives and friends in the U.S. But if moving overseas is on your retirement radar screen, you need to be aware that Uncle Sam has a lot to say about the potential impact on your finances.

"Generally speaking, pensions and annuities that are U.S.-based will be free from tax in a foreign country," says Jane

Bruno, a Fairfax, Virginia, lawyer who worked for the IRS in Germany and who has written a book about U.S. citizens' overseas tax obligations. "Find out if the country (you are moving to) has a treaty with the U.S. If they don't, it is more likely that they will tax any sort of income." You may qualify for a credit on your U.S. taxes for the amount you pay to another country, Bruno says, but there is a catch: "If the other country taxes you at a higher rate than the U.S. would, you will only get a credit up to the (comparable) U.S. rate."

Robert F. Keats, a financial planner in Phoenix, Arizona, warns that, especially if you have a lot of assets, you should make what he calls a "cross-border plan" to avoid potentially exorbitant or "double" taxation that could result if a U.S. citizen retires and lives permanently outside the country. He points to the example of one couple who realized that, unless they made changes in the legal status of their $3.2 million in assets, if one of them passed away, the surviving spouse could be liable for $4 million in estate taxes, part in the U.S. and part in the foreign country.

Here are some of the basic issues affected by federal laws and policy that you should be aware of before taking off to live on your desert island:

Basics

You will, of course, need a U.S. passport as well as a visa from the country in which you want to live. You must apply for the visa before leaving the U.S. When you check with the embassy or consular officials in your future home about a visa, also ask about driver's license requirements. Once you are living overseas, the 260 U.S. consular offices around the world can help you with serious legal, medical, or financial difficulties that may arise.

Income Tax

The taxes you must pay will depend on whether your new home is one of the more than fifty countries that have tax treaties with the U.S. According to the IRS, most tax treaties allow you to exempt nongovernment pensions and annuities, and some investment income, from taxes you must pay to the foreign country. Treaties also help you avoid having some or all of your income taxed twice. In many cases you will qualify for the Foreign Tax Credit, which allows you to deduct some or all of the income taxes you have paid in another country from taxes you owe to Uncle Sam. Be aware that some countries require you to pay income tax on your U.S. Social Security benefits.

If you decide to live in a country that does not have a tax treaty with the U.S., you will be subject to that country's tax laws, so be sure to inform yourself about them before making your final decision on moving.

Medicare
You will not be covered by Medicare if you live outside the U.S. To get health coverage, you'll need to seek out a private insurance company. Some Medigap policies offer emergency coverage while you are traveling overseas, but this will not apply to your routine care if you actually live abroad.

Mortgage Deduction
You may deduct the mortgage interest you pay on your overseas home from your U.S. taxes, just as you would if the house were in the U.S.

Social Security
You may collect your Social Security benefit almost anywhere in the world. (Exceptions are countries with which the U.S. has strained relations, such as North Korea or Cuba.) Depending on where you live, you may choose whether to have your benefit deposited in a U.S. account, in a foreign account, or to receive a check in the mail. Many retirees who live overseas have their benefit deposited into a U.S. bank or brokerage account and draw on it using checks or other types of money transfers. While living overseas you must file regular reports to Social Security on your address, changes in family status, and other

Retiring Outside the U.S.

The following resources will help you get started on planning for retirement in your favorite foreign country:

Passports, Visas, and Other Basics
You may order two free pamphlets, "U.S. Consuls Help Americans Abroad" and "The Office of Overseas Citizens Services," through the Bureau of Consular Affairs of the State Department's fax, 202-647-3000. You may also read these and find many other useful publication at this address on the State Department's website: http://travel.state.gov/acs.html

Social Security
Order the free pamphlet "Your Social Security Payments While You are Out of the Country" from their toll-free line: 1-800-772-1213.

Taxes
Call the Internal Revenue Service's toll-free order line, 1-800-829-3676, to request Publication 54: "Tax Guide for U.S. Citizens and Resident Aliens Abroad." On the Internet, check the publications list at www.irs.gov for additional guidance on information and forms that address international tax issues.

relevant topics. If you are under seventy and work more than forty-five hours per month, Social Security will withhold your benefit for every month that your earnings are not subject to U.S. Social Security taxes.

Voting
As a U.S. citizen, you may vote in federal, state, and local elections even while living outside the country.

Withholding Tax
The IRS requires brokerage houses or other agents to withhold 30 percent of your dividends and interest when they send you the money you've earned on investments. You can avoid this withholding, however, by writing a letter to the agent, explaining that you are a U.S. citizen living abroad and are not subject to the withholding rules that apply to nonresident aliens.

Wills and Estates
People who are living overseas or who own property overseas need to consult with a lawyer who specializes in that country's laws to learn how you can leave your foreign property to heirs in the United States. This may depend on whether the country where you plan to live has signed an international agreement called "Providing a Uniform Law on the Form of an International Will," which governs these situations.

*   *   *

Before you retire, your decisions about where to live most often depend on the requirements or options offered by your employment. Other financial, legal, and personal considerations play a role, but they don't necessarily dominate your decisions.

When you retire, however, the balance among these factors shifts. You'll probably experience a change in the sources and amount of your income, and you may be concerned about physical limitations you have now or may have in the future. But best of all, if you have adequate retirement savings, you will have new freedom to choose your lifestyle based on what you *really* want to do, rather than what your job requires you to do. Instead of limiting your choices, start with an open mind and think about the type of environment that would make you happy and allow you to pursue your personal interests and dreams.

Then go to work on your financial plan, which should include a thorough analysis of the tax and other financial implications of government policies that can make a difference in the type and location of a home you can afford. In that plan, be sure you remember and consider the following ways the federal government may affect your options and, ultimately, your decision:

• Uncle Sam has a myriad of tax rules related to your residence, whether you are buying or selling a home, keeping your current home, or moving to a foreign country;

• Federal law protects you against discrimination on the basis of disability, perceived disability, or in securing financing for a home in the U.S.; and

• No decision you make on a residence is irrevocable. However, before making an investment or completely disrupting your current lifestyle, you should inform yourself about the financial problems you could encounter if you change your mind.

FOR MORE INFORMATION

BY TELEPHONE

AARP
Call 1-800-424-3410 to order a free copy of "Housing" (D 15561), a fact sheet, which explains low-cost housing options and tells you where you can find information about them. You may also order "Selecting Retirement Housing" (D 13680), which describes each type of housing, and "Doable, Renewable Home" (D 12470), which lists ways to make your home more comfortable if you have physical limitations. Also ask for these

two helpful brochures: "Home Safe Home: How to Prevent Falls in the Home (D16598)," and "How Well Does Your Home Meet Your Needs?" (D12670).

AARP Home Equity Information Center (HEIC)

To request a free copy of the forty-eight-page guidebook "Home-Made Money: Consumer's Guide to Home Equity Conversion" (No. D 12894), which discusses the risks and benefits of home equity conversion, call the Publication Hotline at 202-434-6042. You can also order the "Reverse Mortgage Kit," which contains several fact sheets and a current list of reverse mortgage lenders and counselors. HEIC also sells a "Reverse Mortgage Choices Videotape Package" (D 16402), which includes two fifteen-minute, closed-captioned video programs and a resource guide for $5.

American Bar Association Commission on Legal Problems of the Elderly

If you are considering buying or renting a home in a Continuing Care Retirement Community, order a pamphlet, "Retirement Housing Options," which includes an article on "Consumer Contracts for Continuing Care Facilities," by Charles Sabatino. The article will help you evaluate the contract you are being asked to sign. The publication costs $5.00. Call 202-662-8690 for ordering information.

Center for Disease Control and Prevention (CDC), National Center for Injury Prevention and Control

This government agency publishes a free brochure, "Check for Safety: A Home Fall Prevention Checklist for Older Adults." You can order this and other related information from the SAFE USA Hotline, at 1-888-252-7751.

Fannie Mae (FNMA)

To learn about this agency's two types of reverse mortgages, and get a list of lenders who offer them, call 1-800-732-6643 for these free pamphlets: "Home Keeper: It Pays to Keep You in

Your Home" and "Home Keeper for Home Purchase."

Federal Trade Commission (FTC)

This government agency will send you the brochures "Credit and Older Americans" and "Facts for Consumers: Reverse Mortgages." Call 202-326-2222.

Internal Revenue Service (IRS)

In addition to Publication 502, "Medical and Dental Expenses," and Publications 54 and 776 (see the box on page 201 for key references on living overseas), you may also order a free copy of "Tax Guide for U.S. Citizens and Resident Aliens Abroad" (Pub. 54); "Investment Income and Expenses" (Pub. 550) and "Selling Your Home" (Pub. 523) for information on the new tax rules; and "Home Mortgage Interest Deduction" (Pub. 936) by calling the IRS at 1-800-829-3676 (TDD 1-800-829-4059).

Social Security Administration (SSA)

To order the free pamphlet "Your Social Security Payments While You Are Outside the United States (S-10137)," call 1-800-772-1213 (TDD 1-800-325-0778).

U.S. Department of Housing and Urban Development (HUD)

This government agency operates several telephone information lines for people interested in various aspects of federal housing programs.

   • **HUD-approved housing counseling agencies:** For the name of an agency near you that will provide free or low-cost advice, call the HUD Housing Counseling Clearinghouse at 1-800-217-6970 (TDD 1-800-927-9275).

   • **Reverse mortgages and other HUD-insured mortgages:** Call the above number to receive a free "Reverse Mortgage Package," which includes a fact sheet on reverse mortgages, a list of HUD-approved housing counseling agencies and lenders for your state, and the three fact sheets mentioned above under AARP HEIC, or to request information on lenders and other sources of information about HUD-insured mortgages in your community.

• **Senior housing:** HUD's MultiFamily Housing Clearing-house and Complaint Line at 1-800-685-8470 can send you information on "Section 202 housing" for senior citizens and the disabled.

• **Fair housing:** For a free copy of the brochure, "Fair Housing—It's Your Right," which describes illegal housing practices, special protections for people with disabilities, and how to file a charge against someone you believe has discriminated against you, call HUD's Distribution Center at 1-800-767-7468.

• **Other HUD information and programs:** Call HUD's Community Connections, 1-800-998-9999.

BY MAIL

IRS
You can order the following publications that offer advice to Americans residing abroad by writing to: Assistant IRS Commissioner (Int'l.), Att'n: CP:IN:D:CS, 950 L'Enfant Plaza, South, S.W., Washington, DC 20024. The publications are: Pub. 54, "Tax Guide for U.S. Citizens and Resident Aliens Abroad"; Pub. 514: "Foreign Tax Credit for Individuals"; Pub. 593: "Tax Highlights for U.S. Citizens and Residents Going Abroad."

U.S. Department of State (DOS)
Two free State Department pamphlets that will help you plan for retirement overseas are available from the Bureau of Consular Affairs: "U.S. Consuls Help Americans Abroad," which describes services that consular officials can provide while you are traveling or residing abroad; and "The Office of Overseas Citizens Services," which explains how that agency can help you with problems including processing claims for federal benefits if you live outside the country. To order these publications, contact the U.S. Government Printing Office, Superintendent of Documents, Mailstop SSOP, Washington, DC 20402-4328. Copies are also available from Consular Affairs' automated fax at 202-647-3000.

ON THE INTERNET

www.aoa.dhhs.gov/eldractn/homemodif.html
Check here to read information on how to modify your home to make it safer.

www.aarp.org
At AARP's home page, search under the word "housing" to find a variety of useful articles on housing options for retirement.

www.aarp.org/hecc/home.html
At AARP's Home Equity Information Center home page, choose "Basic Facts about Reverse Mortgages," which describes how to compare the costs of these loans. Clicking on "Home Equity Conversion" at the home page, you can find out about property tax deferral for older homeowners and deferred-payment loans for repairing or improving your home.

www.homepath.com
Operated by Fannie Mae, this site provides information on reverse mortgages and other options that could be used to finance or remodel your retirement home.

www.hud.gov
On the home page of the Department of Housing and Urban Development, click on "senior citizens" to find extensive information about housing for seniors, including housing rights and options for financing purchase or remodeling your home.

www.hud.gov/fhe/fheact.html
Read or download the above-mentioned HUD brochure "Fair Housing—It's Your Right."

www.overseasdigest.com
This is one of several sites you can refer to if you need to chat with Americans living abroad or seek information about taxes

and other rules for retiring overseas. Others are www.expatex-change.com and www.liveabroad.com

www.reverse.org
This website, sponsored by the National Center for Home Equity Conversion, allows you to calculate and compare the costs of reverse mortgages offered by different lenders.

http://travel.state.gov
At the home page of the DOS Bureau of Consular Affairs' website, click on "Travel Publications" to read "Tips for Americans Residing Abroad," "U.S. Consuls Help American Abroad," and other publications with tips on living overseas.

CHAPTER NINE

Buyer Beware: Consumer Protections for Retirees

When the telephone salesman told Alice, a retired school teacher, that she could double her money by investing $1,000 a month in a company that secures licenses to operate paging services in major cities, it sounded like a good deal to her. But Alice didn't like the idea of agreeing to spend money over the telephone, so just to make sure, she called the Federal Trade Commission (FTC) to see if they had any information about the company. That call saved her a lot of money. The FTC told her that they had sued this company, and had alleged in the suit that no one who "invested" in this company had ever received any money back.

WHAT YOU NEED TO KNOW ABOUT CONSUMER FRAUD

Every time you make a purchase; every time you use or apply for a credit card, a bank account, or any other form of credit; and every time a stranger tries to sell you something you didn't even know you wanted, you place yourself at risk for consumer fraud. The same is true when you use the Internet as a source of information about consumer products or financial products such as stocks; and when you provide your credit card, Social Security number, or other personal identification numbers to Internet-based businesses.

Senior citizens are prime targets for well-organized telemarketing, investment, and other scams that are intended to rob them of all of their savings and even the Social Security or pension income they need to live on.

One of the reasons for this is that in many cases they do have the money—their retirement savings—that scamsters are after. A report by the U.S. House of Representatives Judiciary Committee, which investigated scams against older people, cites these additional reasons: "many elderly people are lonely and appreciate having someone to talk to, even if that person is asking for money. Others are too polite, or too intimidated, to hang up on their callers." "Operation Senior Sentinel," a campaign conducted by the federal government with the help of the AARP to ferret out and prosecute people who conduct telemarketing fraud, found that more than 78 percent of the victims were fifty-five or older.

You may think that you're too sophisticated to be taken in by professional scam artists. Yet the record is clear. Some crooks are so clever that they can wring money even out of highly educated, professional people. At a hearing in the U.S. Senate, one witness described his father, an eighty-three-year-old retired government engineer, as so "honest, trusting, and innocent" that he spent at least $60,000—all of his savings—and ended up with too little money to pay the taxes on his house. The engineer's mistake? He believed a barrage of telemarketers who said his money would go to the war on drugs or to cancer research, or that he would make money by sending his cash to the "Australian lottery."

Another way that retired and older persons can get into money problems is if they want to get or need to use financial credit. If your spouse dies, or if your only income is from Social Security and/or a pension, you could suddenly find that your credit card is being rejected, or that you can't get a loan that you really need to repair the roof.

What does all of this have to do with Uncle Sam?

A lot. The government, which often works closely with state and local officials on consumer issues, has strong laws and resources you can call on, both to prevent being victimized and to get help if you suspect that someone is taking advantage of you or discriminating against you financially.

How can the government protect you against people who want to take your money and give you nothing in return? How can you make sure that you're not being denied credit just because of your age or because you're on Social Security? To answer these questions, the first thing you need to know is which consumer practices violate the law. Several agencies, including the Federal Trade Commission (FTC) and the Securities and Exchange Commission (SEC), have roles in protecting you from consumer fraud and discrimination.

THE ROLE OF THE FEDERAL TRADE COMMISSION (FTC)
The FTC enforces laws that prohibit unfair, deceptive, or fraudulent consumer practices. This mandate outlaws false claims in advertising, marketing, or otherwise promoting products and services ranging from tobacco and health remedies to "free" trips to the Bahamas.

The FTC has several techniques for fighting consumer fraud, including:

• **Issuing special rules that address a particularly serious or widespread consumer protection issue,** such as the Telemarketing Sales Rule (see the box on page 212).

• **Suing companies or individuals that defraud consumers.** Following the 1999 Christmas season, the FTC required various Internet retailers who had not kept their promises on timely shipping to pay $1.5 million in fines. In another action, the agency charged Internet pharmacies with fraud for advertising that they had their own pharmacy when they really bought prescription drugs from a local drug store.

Some FTC campaigns, however, are directly aimed at protecting seniors. For example, in an effort they called "Field of Schemes," the FTC in 1997 sued companies that had allegedly defrauded people—including many elderly persons—of more than $150 million. In "Operation Senior Sentinel," the FTC worked with the FBI and the Justice Department to charge

The Telemarketing Sales Rules

According to rules established by the Federal Trade Commission (FTC), anyone who calls to make a pitch for you to buy something over the phone must:

- Stop calling if you ask them not to call you;
- Call only between the hours of 8 A.M. and 9 P.M.;
- Tell you that this is a sales call and who is calling before they try to sell you anything;
- Not misrepresent any information about their goods or services; and
- Tell you the total cost of any products or services they're offering, as well as other details about the sale or prize promotion.

It is also illegal for a telemarketer to:

- Withdraw money from your checking account without your express, verifiable authorization;
- Lie to you to get you to pay; or
- Require you to pay for credit repair, "recovery room," or advance-fee loan or credit services until these services have been developed. (Recovery-room operators contact people who have lost money to a previous telemarketing scam and promise that, for a fee, they will recover your money. Advance-fee loans are offered by companies that claim they can guarantee you a loan for a fee paid in advance.)

more than 800 persons with federal telemarketing crimes. So far 240 of those charged have been convicted. If the government recovers money from scammers, some of it, minus an "administrative fee" kept by Uncle Sam, goes to compensate the victims.

- **Providing information to help you figure out whether a product or prize offer is really a scam.** Major examples of this are the Consumer Response Center, which you may call or write to get information or complain about a suspicious business, and more than 150 useful consumer pamphlets that you can order free from the government. Topics of these brochures range from tips on how to buy hearing aids or vacation timeshares to steps you should take to resolve a consumer dispute. If you use the Internet, check www.ftc.gov/bcp/menu-seniors to read any of about 150 brochures on consumer issues. (See "For More Information" to learn how to order FTC publications or make a complaint against a business.)

The FTC also enforces laws that forbid creditors from discriminating against you in financial transactions. An important law for people age sixty-two or older is the Equal Credit Opportunity Act, which:

• **Prohibits a creditor, such as a bank, from denying you credit just because of your age.** However, there is one age-related factor that the creditor is allowed to consider in acting on your application—how close you are to retirement, if that will affect your income. Let's say you're sixty-three years old, and you apply for a twenty-year mortgage to purchase a beachfront vacation home. The bank may ask you about—and is allowed to base its decision on the loan on—the amount of income you will have when you retire at sixty-five.

• **Prohibits a creditor from closing or changing the terms of a joint account solely because your spouse dies.** A joint account, in which the credit is based on the income of both spouses, offers the strongest assurance that the account will not be summarily closed if your spouse dies. It is legal for the creditor to ask you to reapply for such an account if your spouse dies, but the decision on the application must be based on your income and assets, not on your age. If you have a "user account"—one with both of your names on it, but based on the income of only the deceased spouse—the creditor is allowed to close the account.

• **Requires a bank, credit card issuer, or other financial institution to which you are applying for credit to consider your Social Security and pension income in deciding whether to extend credit.** This means that you cannot be denied credit simply because you are not working. The General Electric Capital Corp. found this out some years ago when the FTC charged the company with discriminating against applicants for an "instant credit" program because they were not employed full-time. Under an agreement with the FTC the company paid $275,000 to settle this and other discrimination charges.

THE ROLE OF THE SECURITIES AND EXCHANGE COMMISSION (SEC)

In 1993, the SEC charged Prudential Securities, Inc. (PSI) with, among other things, allowing its sales staff to market limited partnerships in investments including real estate, oil and gas, and airplane leasing to consumers without fully disclosing the risks. As a result of these practices, the SEC said, thousands of consumers lost millions of dollars when the investments went bad. PSI has not admitted or denied the SEC's allegations, but in 1993 the company agreed to set up a process for reimbursing the customers' losses. Since then, more than 110,000 people have collected over $960 million in claims. Many of the victims of this fraud were people who had been counting on the proceeds of the leases to boost their retirement savings or their current retirement income.

Are you one of the many people already retired or planning your retirement who does or will count on investment income to supplement what you get from Social Security and/or a pension? If so, you need to know that the government has special laws and programs—including the laws that the SEC said were broken in the PSI case—designed to prevent you from making costly investment mistakes.

The laws against unfair, deceptive, and fraudulent practices described earlier in this chapter apply to the sale of investments, as well as products and services. But the SEC has additional powers to help you guard against being bilked when you buy most publicly traded stocks, including mutual funds. In addition, the SEC enforces other laws designed to shield you against fraudulent conduct by financial planners and brokers and some other investment advisors. Here's what you need to know:

Most companies that sell stock publicly must file an SEC registration statement that describes the company's properties

Investments That Are Not Required to Register With the SEC

If you purchase stock of a U.S. or foreign company or government that is sold in the U.S. securities markets, you can generally assume that those securities have been registered with and are subject to SEC regulations. However, there are some exceptions, including those on the following list (if you're not sure whether an investment you're considering is registered, contact the Office of Investor Education and Assistance—see the "For More Information" section at the end of this chapter):

- Securities of municipal, state, federal, and other domestic government agencies;
- Securities of charitable institutions and banks;
- Certain private offerings of securities to persons or institutions who have access to the information that registration would disclose; and
- "Small issues" of securities and offerings of "small business investment companies." (This exemption may apply to offerings of less than $5 million or less than $1 million, depending on the type of company involved.)

and business, its management, its financial status, and the stock offering. The SEC can order a company that makes a "deliberate attempt to conceal or mislead"—for example, trying to sell you shares in a business that has no existing operations—to stop the stock offering. Legitimate businesses must also comply with many other SEC rules designed to protect investors, including requirements for corporate reporting, procedures for proxy voting, registration of stock exchanges, and registration of stockbrokers and dealers.

To root out brokers, financial planners, or dealers who may have conflicts of interest or engage in shady investment deals, the SEC requires investment advisors in companies that do $25 million or more in business annually to register with the agency and follow rules against fraudulent conduct. For example, an advisor such as a financial planner must tell you of any conflict of interest he or she may have in working with you, and must open up his or her books and records to SEC investigators periodically. The SEC has the power to order an advisor to stop illegal activities, to fine that person, and to refer him or her to the Justice Department for criminal prosecution. A law that went into effect in 1997 removed the SEC's authority to regulate financial advisors in smaller firms. In these cases, you must take such complaints to your state government—usually to the office that regulates securities.

The agency's Office of Investor Education and Assistance (OIEA) issues consumer publications and responds to public inquiries and complaints about investment offerings and investment advisors. You can get a list of the publications, including "Cold Calling," "Invest Wisely—An Introduction to Mutual Funds," and "Ask Questions—Questions You Should Ask About Your Investments," and also order them from the SEC's toll-free line, 1-800-SEC-0330, or through the website (see "For More Information" at the end of this chapter). You can read many more publications on topics such as certificates of deposit, annuities, and foreign stocks on the website.

The OIEA emphasizes that the agency cannot represent you in court if you believe the law has been broken, but that the tips you provide can alert the SEC to investigate, say, a dubious stock offering or a disreputable investment advisor, and if they are violating the law, put them out of business.

DECISIONS YOU NEED TO MAKE TO PROTECT YOURSELF AGAINST CONSUMER FRAUD AND CREDIT DISCRIMINATION

Now that you have a general idea of what types of consumer practices may be illegal, you'll probably become more sensitive to how you are treated and what the terms are when you are approached to buy something or when you apply for credit. If you detect a suspicious marketing approach or believe a seller is not telling the truth, then you'll have to decide what, if anything, to do about it.

WHAT SHOULD I DO IF I THINK TELEMARKETERS ARE PRESSURING ME TO BUY GOODS OR SERVICES I'M NOT SURE THEY'LL DELIVER?

Consumer experts warn that older people are extremely vulnerable to telemarketing scams. If you are retired, and especially if you are at home a lot to respond personally to the telephone, you could easily become a target.

Lists identifying people by demographic information and zip codes are very broadly sold and used by scammers, explains Jodie Bernstein, director of the FTC Bureau of Consumer Protection in Washington. Or you may get on a target list unwittingly by filling out a form to win a vacation or other prize in a booth at your state fair or at the check-out counter at the local supermarket.

Your first line of defense against sleazy telemarketers is to keep in mind that the smooth-talking, personable caller who inquires sweetly about the state of your health can quickly turn into a high-pressure salesperson, harassing and intimidating you by suggesting you'll lose out on a great bargain unless you send money immediately. Also keep in mind that once a telemarketer has identified you as cooperative, the phone calls and appeals for your money are almost certain to escalate.

The simplest way to deal with a suspicious telemarketer is to tell the caller that, as they are required to do under federal law, they should take you off the calling list. Then hang up the phone. If the calls and appeals persist, you should call the FTC's Consumer Response Center at 1-877-382-4537 to complain. The Center will look into your complaint and compare it with others they have received. The information you offer may help the government track down shady telemarketing operations, which often operate across state borders and may not be known to your local authorities. Alternatively, if you do not want to pay for a long-distance phone call, you may call the consumer affairs office of your city or county, your state attorney general, or the nearest Better Business Bureau.

WHAT SHOULD I DO IF I THINK I HAVE BEEN CHEATED OUT OF MY MONEY?

Did you send money to a telemarketer who promised you a "prize" in return? Some people who were scammed by a convicted crook who revealed his methods to a Senate committee received a "twenty-one-foot boat" that turned out to be a rubber boat with no motor, which cost the telemarketer $4.50. Others paid this crook and his partners in crime anywhere from $75,000 to $100,000 to get a car worth, at most, $7,500.

Did you try to get your money back from an unknown caller who asked you for $960 upfront to help you recover money you lost in a previous scam? (This is known as a "recovery-room" scam.)

Did you respond to an Internet offer to invest in a coconut plantation in Costa Rica and then find out that it did not exist?

These are all true examples of situations you should report, both to help the government shut down these types of frauds and to try to get back the money you, personally, have lost. What should you do in these cases?

IF YOU RECEIVED A PRIZE, A PRODUCT, OR A SERVICE THAT WAS WORTH LESS THAN YOU WERE PROMISED, REPORT IT TO THE FTC CONSUMER RESPONSE CENTER (SEE PAGE 217).

The FTC may be able to tell you if a suit is pending against the company or individual or if legal action has taken place and— although this is rare—if a fund has already been established for compensating victims. If the FTC has an ongoing investigation, however, the agency cannot tell you about it. Your state attorney general, state or local consumer affairs office, or Better Business Bureau, however, may be able to provide more information if they have received other complaints about the operator and/or if any action has been taken.

IF YOU BOUGHT STOCK IN A CROOKED COMPANY, OR
YOU BELIEVE YOUR BROKER SOLD YOU A BAD INVEST-
MENT BY GIVING YOU MISINFORMATION, COMPLAIN
BY WRITING OR CALLING THE SEC'S OFFICE OF
INVESTOR EDUCATION AND ASSISTANCE.

As a result of such reports, the SEC may be able to shut down
these fraudulent operations. If your complaint is about a local
financial advisor, however, you may want to contact your state
securities regulators or consumer office first, because they may
be more knowledgeable about someone in your area. To pursue
your own case and try to get money back from a bad investment, you will have to hire a lawyer. Keep in mind, however,
that the SEC cannot represent you in a lawsuit.

WHAT SHOULD I DO IF I SUSPECT THAT A CREDITOR
HAS TURNED ME DOWN FOR A CREDIT CARD, AN
ACCOUNT, OR A LOAN BECAUSE OF MY AGE OR
BECAUSE MY ONLY INCOME IS FROM SOCIAL
SECURITY AND PENSIONS?

Start by asking the creditor to explain why you were rejected. You
have a right under the Equal Credit Opportunity Act to receive a
statement of the specific reasons why your application was
denied. If the reason appears to be based on your age or failure to
consider Social Security income, write to the federal agency that
oversees the bank or other credit institution. The name of the federal agency should be in the letter you receive rejecting your
application. If not, the company is violating the law.

Most retired people live on limited incomes from Social
Security, pensions, and savings. Unless you are fortunate enough to
build up a lot of resources, either from a large salary or clever investing, you need to be vigilant about how you spend your money.

The financial resources of retired people, unfortunately, are
at risk. You can suffer losses from a number of sources: organ-
ized, fraudulent operators who promise you "prizes," "awards,"
or astronomical returns on investments; unsavory brokers or
other investment advisors who may give you advice that is more

in their interest than in your own; and businesses or financial institutions that do not want your business because they don't trust retirees to manage their money responsibly.

*   *   *

You can protect yourself against these types of assaults on your financial resources by learning about, and taking advantage of, federal consumer protection laws, and by resisting tempting offers from strangers whose credentials you cannot check out yourself. The key points to remember are:

• The federal government regulates telemarketing and gives you the legal right to have your name taken off the phone lists used by telemarketers.

• If an offer to buy a product or service or win a prize sounds suspicious, "just say no." Then report the suspicious come-on to the Consumer Response Center (see page 217).

• Even if you have a broker or other financial advisor, monitor your investments very closely, on a regular basis. Be aware of the problem of "churning," in which an investment manager conducts frequent sales transactions that generate lots of commissions but few earnings for you. Use the publications and other resources of the Securities and Exchange Commission to make sure your money is being managed in your own interest.

• Know your rights to credit as a retired person. If a bank or other institution tries to deny you a credit card or loan, check with the FTC to see if this is legal under the Equal Credit Opportunity Act.

FOR MORE INFORMATION

BY TELEPHONE

Federal Trade Commission (FTC)
To complain about a business or a business practice, call the FTC's Consumer Response Center at 1-877-382-4357. Call 1-202-326-2222 to order "Best Sellers," a list of the FTC's free

consumer publications, such as "Credit and Older Americans" and "Are You a Target of Telephone Scams?"

General Services Administration
The "2001 Consumer Action Handbook" is a 144-page guide, complete with addresses and phone numbers, to federal and state consumer offices and private consumer groups to which you can report suspected fraud or complain about consumer issues. It also includes features such as tips on avoiding fraud and protecting your privacy. You can order a free copy by calling 1-888-878-3256.

Securities and Exchange Commission (SEC)
Call 1-800-732-0330 to ask questions or complain about investments or investment advisors. You can also order free publications, including "What Every Investor Should Know," "Ask Questions: Questions You Should Ask About Your Investments," and "Investment Fraud in Cyberspace." To order a list of SEC publications, call 1-202-942-7040.

BY MAIL

AARP
You may order free information on how to protect yourself against fraud by writing to AARP Fulfillment EE01196, 601 E St. N.W., Washington, DC 20049. Ask for the "AARP Bulletin Special Report—Telemarketing Fraud" (stock number D16604).

FTC
To order "Best Sellers" and the other free pamphlets mentioned above, write to the FTC's Consumer Response Center, 600 Pennsylvania Ave., NW, Room H-130, Washington, DC 20580.

SEC
Address questions and complaints to the SEC's Office of Investor Education and Assistance, at 450 Fifth St. N.W., Washington, DC 20549.

ON THE INTERNET

www.consumer.gov
Here you'll find encyclopedic resources on a range of consumer issues that affect current and future retirees.

www.ftc.gov
This website contains the full text of FTC consumer publications on topics such as consumer credit, investments, and telemarketing.

www.pueblo.gsa.gov
From this site you can download more than two hundred consumer publications, including the "2001 Consumer Action Handbook" described above.

www.sec.gov
You can look up corporate information such as annual reports on the SEC's EDGAR Database. If you have a complaint against a broker or other financial services purveyor, you can file it online at this website. In addition, you can read many of the Office of Investor Education's publications with consumer tips on everything from margin trading to buying CDs, or order copies of those that are not available online.

Uncle Sam's Ten Best Retirement Websites

www.aoa.dhhs.gov
The Administration on Aging website will update you on issues such as caregiving and assistance for seniors, and new publications or policies on health or retirement issues.

www.consumer.gov
This is the gateway to consumer information and publications from all over the government.

www.dol.gov/dol/pwba
Read or order publications about your pension rights and employee health benefits.

www.firstgov.gov
This site allows you to search the entire federal government on topics ranging from health care issues to taxes and much more.

www.health.gov
Look here for information on topics such as the latest health research, particular diseases and treatments, and nutrition tips.

www.irs.gov
The definitive tax information source allows you to both read and order tax publications online.

www.medicare.gov
The Medicare website offers publications explaining the program's costs and benefits. By using "Medicare Compare," or "Nursing Home Compare," features, you can get information to compare the options for Medicare coverage and nursing home care in your area.

www.search.pbgc.gov
Here's the place to look for a pension you may have lost or forgotten about.

www.seniors.gov
A good place to start if you need information specifically relating to retirement. Links to Social Security, Medicare, and much more.

www.ssa.gov
At the Social Security Administration website, you can order an estimate of your future benefit, calculate the best retirement date for yourself and get answers to your questions about how Social Security works.

Tax Checklists for Future and Current Retirees

Almost every year, Congress passes and the President approves some major tax laws that change some of the rules affecting your retirement planning or your current retirement income.

Because of these constant changes, a basic rule prevails: virtually every financial move you make has an impact on your tax bill and therefore on your income and, potentially, on the choices you man make about your lifestyle. Each chapter in this book pinpoints the most important tax implications of retirement-related decisions in a specific area, such as Social Security or long-term care. This section summarizes the key tax rules already described and adds a few more that have not already been discussed, including the basic policies on making gifts and transferring other assets that you need to know for estate planning.

These lists are not comprehensive, and the rules that determine if you must pay a certain tax or if you qualify for a deduction, credit, or exclusion from your income are often based on complex formulas. *The higher your income and the more complicated your financial situation is, the more likely it is that you need an expert tax advisor to make sure you minimize what you owe and maximize your benefits.*

To get an idea of the range of tax issues you need to know about, you can use these checklists in the following way:

• Pick the one that best describes your current status and review the list of taxes and tax breaks that may apply to you;

• Request and read the IRS publications that explain the rules in detail; or

• Work with a financial advisor on a current or future retirement budget that will be the best for you and your family.

CHECKLIST NUMBER ONE:
IF YOU ARE WORKING AND PLANNING FOR RETIREMENT

The taxes and tax breaks listed here have a direct relationship to planning or saving for retirement. The list does not include tax policies that are not directly related to retirement, such as routine family medical expenses or the home mortgage deduction.

WHAT YOU PAY

- Income tax on wages or self-employment income: amount of income determines amount of tax-favored contributions you can make to retirement savings.
- Capital gains taxes on profits from investments, including stocks, bonds, and real estate.
- FICA tax to pay for your Social Security and Medicare.
- Income tax on a loan you take from your 401(k).

WHAT YOU CAN DEDUCT OR EXCLUDE FROM INCOME

Business Expenses
If your retirement preparations include developing a sideline business or moonlighting while you still work at your regular job, you can deduct:

- If you are employed, the cost of unreimbursed business expenses, including job-related education, dues to professional groups or a union, malpractice insurance, etc.
- If you are self-employed, your business expenses for office rental and utilities, supplies, transportation, meals and entertainment, etc.
- Home office expenses (based on strict criteria).

Medical Expenses
- Contributions to a Medical Savings Account (MSA).
- If your medical expenses exceed 7.5 percent of your adjusted gross income: part of the premium you pay for long-term-care insurance.
- Expenses for care of an invalid parent or other dependent in your home (Child and Dependent Care Credit).

Retirement Savings
- Contributions to a 401(k), deductible IRA, SEP, Keogh, SIMPLE, or other tax-favored retirement savings plan.

Transfers of Gifts and Assets
- Lifetime transfers of gifts and assets in your estate of $675,000 for 2001, with indexing up to $1 million in 2006 and thereafter.
- Gifts of up to $10,000 per year (to be indexed for inflation in $1,000 increments) to, for example, your children or other heirs.
- "Generation-skipping" transfers of up to $1 million in assets, to, for example, your grandchildren. (This went into effect on December 31, 1998, and is indexed for inflation, in increments of $10,000, for each year thereafter.)

PENALTIES
- If you are younger than fifty-nine and a half, a 10 percent penalty on money you withdraw from tax-favored retirement savings including your 401(k), IRA, SEP, or Keogh (unless the money is withdrawn for limited, allowed purchases, including purchasing a home for the first time).
- Withdrawals from a SIMPLE plan if you are younger than fifty-nine and a half and you have participated in the plan for less than two years—a penalty of 25 percent in addition to the income tax.

CHECKLIST NUMBER TWO:
IF YOU ARE WORKING IN RETIREMENT

This list contains taxes and tax breaks that apply to people who are retired, receiving a pension and/or Social Security, and who also continue to work.

WHAT YOU PAY

- Income tax on wages or self-employment income.
- Income tax on the money you receive from a pension and/or, if you exceed the annual "earnings limit," on your income from Social Security.
- Income tax on all or part of the regular income you receive from an annuity.
- If you are fifty-nine and a half or older and leave your job, income tax on the "lump sum distributions" you receive when you take all the money out of your employer's tax-favored pension plan.
- If you are fifty-nine and a half or older, income tax on money you take out of a traditional IRA (to the extent that you have not already paid taxes on it), SEP, SIMPLE, or Keogh plan.
- Capital gains taxes on profits on investments including stocks, bonds, and real estate.
- FICA tax on earnings from your work.

TAX CREDITS

- If you have a job and pay for the care for your spouse or other dependent who has a physical or mental impairment to caring for him- or herself, and that person lives in your home, you may be eligible for a tax credit for some of the costs of the care (Child and Dependent Care Credit).
- People over sixty-five whose income falls within certain limits may be eligible for the Tax Credit for the Elderly or the Disabled. (If you are disabled, you may be eligible if you are

younger than sixty-five.) The income limits are based on your filing status.

WHAT YOU CAN DEDUCT OR EXCLUDE FROM INCOME

Standard Deduction: If you are sixty-five or older, you may claim a higher standard deduction than younger taxpayers. In 2000, the standard deduction for a single person or head of household was $4,400; for a married couple filing jointly it was $7,350. People who were over sixty-five or who were blind, however, could deduct $6,600. A married couple, filing jointly, could deduct $9,050.

Business Expenses

- If you are employed, the cost of unreimbursed business expenses, including job-related education, dues to professional groups or a union, malpractice insurance, etc.
- If you are self-employed, your business expenses for office rental and utilities, supplies, transportation, meals and entertainment, etc.
- Home office expenses (based on strict criteria).

Medical Expenses

- Contributions to a Medical Savings Account (MSA).
- If you are self-employed: 60 percent of the cost of the premium you pay for health insurance in 2000, increasing gradually to 100 percent in 2003 and thereafter.
- If your medical expenses exceed 7.5 percent of your adjusted gross income:
  —part of the premium you pay for long-term-care insurance;
  —benefits you receive from long-term-care insurance, up to $200 per day in 2001;
  —some or part of the cost of improving or remodeling your home for medical reasons.
- Expenses for care of an invalid spouse or other dependent in your home (Child and Dependent Care Credit).

Retirement Home

- Home mortgage deduction for current or new home, including residence outside the U.S.
- Deduction for remodeling expenses required for medical reasons. (See medical expenses.)

Retirement Savings

- If you are younger than seventy and a half; contributions to a 401(k), deductible IRA, SEP, Keogh, or other tax-favored retirement savings plan.
- A loss on the value of a lump-sum distribution from your employer's tax-favored pension plan.

Transfers of Gifts and Assets

- Lifetime transfers of gifts and assets in your estate of $675,000 in 2001, with indexing up to $1 million in 2006 and thereafter.
- Gifts of up to $10,000 per year (to be indexed for inflation in $1,000 increments), to, for example, your children or other heirs.
- "Generation-skipping" transfers of up to $1 million in assets, to, for example, your grandchildren. (This went into effect on December 31, 1998, and is indexed for inflation, in increments of $10,000, for each year thereafter.)

PENALTIES

- Withdrawals from a SIMPLE plan if you are younger than fifty-nine and a half and you have participated in the plan for less than two years—a penalty tax of 25 percent in addition to the income tax.
- If you are younger than fifty-nine and a half, a 10 percent penalty on money you withdraw from tax-favored retirement money savings including your 401(k), IRA, SEP, or Keogh (unless the money is withdrawn for limited, allowed purposes, including purchasing a home for the first time).

CHECKLIST NUMBER THREE:
IF YOU ARE FULLY RETIRED

WHAT YOU PAY

- Regular income tax on your pension and possibly on a portion of your Social Security benefit.
- Capital gains taxes on profits on investments including stocks, bonds, and real estate.
- If you are fifty-nine and a half or older or leave your job, income tax on the "lump sum distribution" you receive when you take all the money out of your employer's tax-favored pension plan.
- Income tax on all or part of the regular income you receive from an annuity.
- If you are fifty-nine and a half or older, income tax on money you take out of a 401(k), traditional IRA (to the extent that you have not already paid taxes on it), SEP, SIMPLE, or Keogh plan.

TAX CREDITS

- If you have a job and pay for the care for your spouse or other dependent who has a physical or mental impairment that prevents him or her from caring for him- or herself, and that person lives in your home, you may be eligible for a tax credit for some of the costs of the care (Child and Dependent Credit).
- People over sixty-five whose income falls within certain limits may be eligible for the Tax Credit for the Elderly or the Disabled. (If you are disabled, you may be eligible if you are younger than sixty-five.) The income limits are based on your filing status.

WHAT YOU CAN DEDUCT OR EXCLUDE FROM INCOME

Standard Deduction: If you are sixty-five or older, you may claim a higher standard deduction than younger taxpayers. In 2000, the standard deduction for a single person or head of household was $4,400; for a married couple filing jointly it was $7,350. People who were over sixty-five or who were blind, however, could deduct $6,600. A married couple, filing jointly, could deduct $9,050.

Medical Expenses
- Contributions to a Medical Savings Account (MSA).
- If your medical expenses exceed 7.5 percent of your adjusted gross income:
  —part of the premium you pay for long-term-care insurance;
  —benefits you receive from long-term-care insurance, up to $200 per day in 2001;
  —some or part of the cost of improving or remodeling your home for medical reasons.
- Expenses for care of an invalid spouse or other dependent in your home (Child and Dependent Care Credit).

Retirement Home
- Home mortgage deduction for current or new home, including residence outside the U.S.
- Deduction for remodeling expenses required for medical reasons. (See medical expenses.)

Retirement Savings
- A loss on the value of a lump-sum distribution from your employer's tax-favored pension plan.

Transfers of Gifts and Assets
- Lifetime transfers of gifts and assets in your estate of $675,000 in 2001, with indexing up to $1 million in 2006 and thereafter.
- Gifts of up to $10,000 per year (to be indexed for inflation in $1,000 increments), to, for example, your children or other heirs.
- "Generation-skipping" transfers of up to $1 million in

assets, to, for example, your grandchildren. (This went into effect on December 31, 1998, and is indexed for inflation, in increments of $10,000, for each year thereafter.)

• Withdrawals from a SIMPLE plan if you are younger than fifty-nine and a half and you have participated in the plan for less than two years—a penalty tax of 25 percent in addition to the income tax.

• If you are younger than fifty-nine and a half, a 10 percent penalty on money you withdraw from tax-favored retirement money savings including your 401(k), IRA, SEP, or Keogh (unless the money is withdrawn for limited, allowed purposes, including purchasing a home for the first time).

FOR MORE INFORMATION

You may order the following free publications by calling the Internal Revenue Service toll-free number, 1-800-829-3676.

You may also research tax questions through the IRS website at www.irs.gov/.

GENERAL TAX INFORMATION
Miscellaneous Deductions (Pub. 529)
Older Americans Tax Guide (Pub.554)
Tax Guide for Small Business (Pub. 334)
Tax Guide for U.S. Citizens and Resident Aliens Abroad (Pub. 54)
Your Federal Income Tax (Pub. 17)

BUSINESS EXPENSES AND DEDUCTIONS
Business Use of Your Home (Pub. 587)
Self-Employment Tax (Pub. 533)
Tax Guide for Small Business (Pub. 334)
Travel, Entertainment, Gift, and Car Expenses (Pub. 463)

MEDICAL EXPENSES
Medical and Dental Expenses (Pub. 502)

RETIREMENT HOME
Home Mortgage Interest Deduction (Pub. 963)
Selling Your Home (Pub. 523)

RETIREMENT INCOME
Pension and Annuity Income (Pub. 575)
Social Security and Equivalent Railroad Retirement Benefits (Pub. 915)
Tax Guide to U.S. Civil Service Retirement Benefits (Pub. 721)

RETIREMENT SAVINGS
Individual Retirement Arrangements (Pub. 590)
Retirement Plans for Small Businesses (Pub. 560)

TAX CREDITS
Credit for the Elderly or the Disabled (Pub. 524)
Child and Dependent Care Expenses (Pub. 503)

TRANSFERRING GIFTS AND ASSETS
Introduction to Estate and Gift Taxes (Pub. 950)

INDEX

About the Author

Ellen Hoffman is a freelance writer, author, and speaker on retirement and personal finance topics. Her other book on retirement, *The Retirement Catch-up Guide*, was also published by Newmarket Press.

A veteran Washington reporter, Ellen has extensive experience in covering issues including Social Security, Medicare, long-term care, and the impact of tax policy on retirement. Currently she is the retirement columnist for *Business Week Online* and writes often for *Business Week* magazine.

A former *Washington Post* reporter, Ellen was the Washington columnist for "Retire With Money," a newsletter formerly published by *Money* magazine. Her articles have also appeared in *Money, Kiplinger's Retirement Report, Reader's Digest New Choices for Better Living After 50, Modern Maturity,* and many other national magazines and newspapers.

Ellen has appeared on NBC's *Today Show*, on CNBC, Fox News, NPR's *Morning Edition*, Bloomberg's Spanish-language radio, and many other television and radio shows all over the country to talk about retirement. She's been a featured speaker at money management conferences sponsored by *The Washington Post* and *The Miami Herald* newspapers, and many other conferences and seminars.

Personal Finance/Retirement Books From Newmarket Press

ELLEN HOFFMAN

The Retirement Catch-Up Guide
54 Real-Life Lessons to Boost Your Future Resources Now!
Real stories. Real People. Real strategies. Here's how these late starters made up for lost time and how you too can catch up on your financial planning for retirement.

"A jam packed guide filled with common sense advice, countless resources, and personal anecdotes."—Don Blandin, President, American Savings Education Council

Bankroll Your Future Retirement With Help from Uncle Sam—2nd Edition
How Government Perks and Policies Can Affect Your Income, Your Healthcare, Your Home, and Your Assets

"An invaluable resource for every American planning for a secure retirement." —Senator William V. Roth, Jr., Chairman, Senate Finance Committee

SUZE ORMAN

You've Earned It, Don't Lose It ®
Mistakes You Can't Afford to Make When You Retire
Over 500,000 copies sold! Orman's only book specifically on retirement, this covers investment advice, trusts vs. wills, joint tenancy and gifting, power of attorney, long-term-care insurance, early retirement, and more. From the author of the #1 *New York Times* bestsellers *The Courage to Be Rich* and *The 9 Steps to Financial Freedom*.

Books are available from your local bookstore, or use this coupon. Enclose a check or money order payable to **Newmarket Press** and send to: Newmarket Press, 18 E. 48th St., New York, NY 10017. Credit card orders: **1-800-669-3903** or **1-800-233-4830**

I enclose a check or money order payable to Newmarket Press in the amount of _____

Name _____

_____

Address _____

_____

_____

City/State/Zip _____

E-mail _____

quantity	title	amount
	Bankroll Your Future Retirement, 2nd Ed.	
_____	$16.95 pb (1-55704-411-2) . . . . .$	_____
	The Retirement Catch-Up Guide	
_____	$22.95 hc (1-55704-411-2) . . . . .$	_____
	You've Earned It, Don't Lose It	
_____	$15.00 pb (1-55704-316-7) . . . . .$	_____
_____	$24.00 hc (1-55704-322-1) . . . . .$	_____
_____	$19.95 audio book (1-55704-285-3) $	_____
	*Plus shipping and handling $	_____
	NYS Residents add 8.25% Sales Tax $	_____
	TOTAL AMOUNT ENCLOSED $	_____

*Shipping & Handling. Add $3.00 for the first item, and $1.00 for each additional item. Allow 4-6 weeks for delivery. Prices and availability are subject to change without notice.

For discounts on orders of five or more copies or to get a catalog, contact Newmarket Press, Special Sales Department, 18 East 48th Street, New York, NY 10017; phone 212-832-3575 or 800-669-3903 fax 212-832-3629; or e-mail sales@newmarketpress.com

BOB.BYRF.03